THE
INTERNATIONAL ADOPTION
HANDBOOK

THE
INTERNATIONAL
ADOPTION
HANDBOOK

*How to Make an
Overseas Adoption
Work for You*

MYRA ALPERSON

An Owl Book
Henry Holt and Company
New York

Owl Books
Henry Holt and Company, LLC
Publishers since 1866
175 Fifth Avenue
New York, New York 10010
www.henryholt.com

An Owl Book® and 🐦® are registered trademarks
of Henry Holt and Company, LLC.

Library of Congress Cataloging-in-Publication Data
Alperson, Myra.
The international adoption handbook: how to make an overseas adoption
work for you / Myra Alperson. — 1st ed.
        p.   cm.
Includes bibliographical references and index.
ISBN-13: 978-0-8050-4579-6
ISBN-10: 0-8050-4579-1
1. Intercountry adoption—United States—Handbooks, manuals, etc.
2. Interracial adoption—United States—Handbooks, manuals, etc.
3. Adoptive parents—United States—Psychology—Handbooks,
manuals, etc.   I. Title.
HV875.5.A435   1997   96-39053
362.7'34—dc20   CIP

Henry Holt books are available for special promotions and
premiums. For details contact: Director, Special Markets.

Designed by Kate Nichols

Printed in the United States of America

P1

To my parents and my daughter

Contents

PART II
*A New Beginning: Issues and Experiences
of International Adoption*

Acknowledgments

One Saturday evening, early in my adoption process, I came to the monthly meeting of the Adoptive Parents Committee (APC), which is held at a local college in my area. I usually went there with a friend, but I was alone that night. After an early workshop, I joined the plenary session in a large auditorium where families that had completed adoptions during the previous month were brought to the stage with their new children. It is a wonderful moment, especially if you recognize the faces of people who have been waiting for so long for their children. At a certain moment I started crying. A woman sitting nearby saw me and put her arm around me. "You *will* have a child," she said. She already had completed an adoption and came to APC for its postadoption workshops. Her gesture helped enormously.

That type of warmth and outreach is typical of the generosity of many people who have adopted children and know what those of us still going through it are feeling. So I want, first of all, to thank the people at APC. You will likely be helped by people like that woman. Some will become your friends while others will pass through your life just briefly. They all make a difference.

I hadn't planned to write an adoption book. But since I am a writer and since I was adopting, my friend and agent, Gareth Esersky, of the Carol Mann Agency in New York City, urged me to put together a proposal. It wasn't hard to do; when you're adopting, you're learning much of it on the spot. I had a tremendous additional amount of research to do, but it wasn't very hard to find. And Gareth found me an excellent publisher. So I must also acknowledge her.

Working with a good editor is a great privilege, and I had the privilege of working with Cynthia Vartan, herself an adoptive mother. She was particularly supportive when I delayed starting the book because of a glitch in my own adoption—a fairly common occurrence in international adoptions—which temporarily kept me from writing.

Alliance for Children, the agency I worked with, was always helpful and responsive. When my first application was lost in the mail—they never got it and it was never returned to me—they Fed-Exed a new one immediately so that I had it in my hands first thing the next morning. When my referral came through but the trip to China was delayed, Alliance kept reassuring me with information and, at one point, audiocassettes from other parents describing their own adoption experience in Suzhou, the city my daughter is from. Alliance (and, particularly, Ruthie Rich) was always there for me.

Miriam Vieni is the extraordinary social worker whose wit and insights helped me decide that I could adopt and also how to adopt. I had been thinking about adoption for a long time but had done nothing about it. When I told Miriam I was thinking about doing a book, she asked me how I would know that the book was accurate and to the point. "If you review it, I will," I said. She agreed. Her contribution and time were invaluable. She also provided useful parenting advice.

Like many parents who adopt, I had originally hoped to have

a biological child. Things didn't quite work out as I had thought. But look at how they *have* worked out! Adoption is a gift that is hard to describe in words. I have tried to use words to explain the planning and process leading to adoption, but it is difficult to find the words to capture the impact and experience adoption has had on my life.

My parents, Leo and June Alperson, have been extraordinary through my adoption, from the day that I told them that I was considering it to the day that it finally happened and I brought my daughter home. They laughed and cried with me. They reassured me that any child of mine would be loved by them, and that has been the case. My sister, brother, and sister-in-law, Ruth, Phil, and Jane, have also been there all along. So has my nephew, Jeremy. My good friend Nan Rubin deserves extra mention for offering to join me in China, since I would no doubt need help and moral support. I did. Thanks, Nan!

And there's Sadie. Somewhere there is a woman who gave birth to Sadie. She has given me a gift. I would like somehow for her to know this some day.

I have interspersed the experiences of a number of adoptive families throughout this book, some in considerable detail. These households reflect the diversity of the types of adoptions and families that adopt. Some are headed by couples, others by single parents. Some families have other adopted children, or have birth children and adopted children. They live in cities, suburbs, and exurbs, in large houses and small apartments. Many work full-time, but there are some stay-at-home parents and a few free-lancers. Some parents have adopted children who have disabilities, while others knew that they could not do this; some sought infants, others older children. Some used agencies, others arranged their adoptions through facilitators.

I have changed the names of most of them at their request to protect their confidentiality, but I wish to thank them for taking the time to share their stories. In a few cases, however, people I interviewed gave me permission to use their real names and describe their experiences. They include Susan and Hector Badeau and their family, which I had the joyful opportunity to visit twice; Judi Kloper and Peter Owens and their children (whom I have "met" through E-mail, telephone, and "snail mail"); and Wayne Steinman, a fellow New Yorker. A heartfelt, special thanks to all of them—we have also become friends. Hearing about adoption through the experiences of others is the best way to learn about how it actually happens and how to make the process work for you.

Introduction

You and I Have a Few Things in Common

If you've already begun skimming through books on adoption, you'll realize that many authors are adoptive parents themselves, as I am. I am the adoptive mother of a Chinese-born girl. She came into my life in 1996 after a long process that I would have to say began sometime in the late 1980s when I was involved in a relationship that I thought would lead to marriage and children.

The relationship ended, and I then found myself where you may well be now: sad not to have children (or perhaps more children) and tired of feeling hurt at seeing friends' families grow and watching other people's children in the park. I loved the children's sections of bookstores, but I also resented them because I felt that when I entered them, I was trespassing into illicit territory since I didn't have the proper passport: a child of my own.

I initially convinced myself that I didn't really want children after all. If I did, I'd *have* them, right? Then I had to admit that I was fooling myself: Of course I *did* want a child. I *wanted* to hug a baby that was my own. I wanted to experience *my* child's first steps and words. I wanted to walk a child to school and read that child to sleep. I wanted to go to school plays and give my child music lessons and marvel at my child's accomplishments, whether they were in school, sports, the arts, or whatever she chose to pursue. I wanted to help that child become a fulfilled, responsible adult. I wanted to be called "Mom."

The Adoption Option

I already knew that I did not want to give birth on my own. Why should I, when there were so many homeless children? Although I had once dreamed of giving birth with a partner, it seemed like a lonely experience to go through without one. So I thought about adopting.

I talked to people. I went to bookstores and thumbed through books on adoption—and bought a few. I made a checklist of the names of adoption agencies in the Yellow Pages. I found out about adoption magazines and newsletters. I surfed the Internet and discovered a world of adoption information available, literally, at my fingertips. Before long I started going to adoption seminars.

At these seminars I bumped into people I'd known years earlier: old friends or former colleagues. Some were married, some weren't. Some had had children biologically and wanted to expand their families. Others were just starting. And I made new friends: people like me who were embarking on a new and sometimes scary adventure.

Deciding to Adopt Internationally

The decision to adopt internationally came surprisingly easily. I was over forty and knew that a U.S. adoption was unlikely unless I was willing to adopt an older child or a child who had special needs.

As a single woman with a full-time job and a profession that I love, I didn't feel I could do this. And besides, I had always wanted a baby. Why should I stop wanting one now? Going overseas to adopt a younger, healthier child, I learned, was the best option to realize this dream. Also, I learned, adopting a United States–born infant was often far more expensive than going overseas. This was a consideration for me.

More than that, though, I became intrigued with the opportunity of raising a child whose birth culture was different from mine. The longer I thought about it, the more the idea became an enticing way to enrich my own life by learning about the country my child-to-be came from while I would hope to share my background with my child.

Becoming Informed

But I needed to get good information. There was *so* much to be had—and, it seemed to me, not enough time to sort through it. And much of the information was conflicting. Could I adopt in a particular country or couldn't I? Would it cost $10,000 or $25,000? Would I have to travel or could the child be escorted to the United States? Were there religious requirements? Did I need to have a large home in order to adopt a child? Would I have to take *two* trips for the child? How would I choose the right agency? Did I need a lawyer? Did it really take *years* for a foreign adoption to be completed? Would I need to change jobs and earn more money? And on and on . . .

Why I Wrote This Book: To Help You Become Organized and Make the Right Decisions

I learned a lot as the result of my experience—and I've made some mistakes along the way, too. I've written this book to guide you toward an effective international adoption, building both on what I learned and also on where I stumbled. I've done this in a straightforward manner.

Here's What This Book *Does:*

- Demystifies international adoption with *step-by-step* guidelines to get you going.
- Provides *current information on resources* that can help you make the best decisions.
- Offers suggestions on how to finance your adoption.
- Answers many common questions regarding international adoption, based on interviews with adoptive families and adoption professionals.
- Recommends adoption resources, including support organizations, books, and other sources of information as you begin your new life as an adoptive parent.

However, This Book *Doesn't* Provide Lists of Adoption Agencies, Fees, or Specific Adoption Programs.

Here's why:

- Agency programs change frequently and agency requirements vary from state to state.
- Fee structures also change often, and they vary with the type of adoption.
- So do the laws in countries where adoptions take place (and so do some laws in the United States that affect

adoption). You may wish to adopt in a particular country, only to learn that adoptions in that country have been put on hold or that new restrictions have been imposed.

I have, however, provided you with the *essential sources of information* on directories of agencies that assist with international adoptions and guidelines on how to select the agency that will give you the best services.

Feeling Comfortable with the Decisions You Make

Nowadays, especially, as many more adoption resources are available, you should be able to get solid information and complete an adoption that will meet your needs as parents-to-be. There may be some glitches—these things *do* happen. But you should be able to link up with an agency or facilitator who truly has *your* best interests in mind and keeps you informed every step of the way.

Look at it this way: in 1995, almost 9,700 children from other countries were placed with U.S. families. International adoptions DO work, and you CAN do it. But do it right! Use this book well, and it should help you enable the adoption process to work for you. And good luck!

PART I

---

*The Nuts and
Bolts of International
Adoption*

1

Making the Choice

If you think international adoption is hard or near impossible, just think of this: close to ten thousand children born outside of the United States are adopted each year by U.S. families. The annual number has been relatively stable for years, hovering between 7,500 and 9,800 adoptions (see table on pages 8–9).

I predict that number will rise to over ten thousand in 1996, and while it won't skyrocket, international adoption will continue to grow—slowly—and become more common. It's not as difficult to do as it used to be; more countries now have the mechanism to place abandoned children with families that want them, and our increasingly diverse society is more receptive to children who are "different."

After all, the typical nuclear family just isn't so common anymore. (Think of all the "alternative" families that now populate network TV.) Many adopters these days are single, like me, and there are books and support groups just for us. Many are older—some in their fifties—as the mother- and fatherhood age ceiling rises (me, too; I'm over forty). Gay couples are forming families through adoption; and in some cases, couples on their "second-go-round" in marriage, who maybe missed out on children their first time out, are turning to adoption to create families.

The news media and technology have had a lot to do with the increasing openness of international adoption. The world is getting smaller. We learn about countries we never knew existed, and hear on the radio or TV about children from there who have lost their parents or about the overcrowded orphanages they live in. A story on National Public Radio in 1995 about a disabled little boy in a Russian orphanage led to a couple in Ohio adopting him. The new father, hearing the story while in his car, said he just "knew" he had to adopt the child. Could this have taken place even five years earlier? Probably not.

A Tradition . . . a More Recent History

Adoption has a long tradition.[1] Remember Moses? You might call that foster care, but yes, that was an adoption. In royal families where there were no male heirs, a nephew might be adopted in order to maintain the family name.

But the types of adoptions I'm writing about here—adoptions of children from overseas by U.S. families—basically goes back to the early 1950s, when a man in Oregon named Harry Holt sought to find homes for Korean war orphans. He eventually founded one of the first U.S. agencies to do international placements, and these days, agencies as well as facilitators (individuals or groups of people not licensed to act as formal agents) help match children needing homes with couples and single people wanting to form families. The children come from all over:

---

[1] Some of the information for this chapter has been drawn from a 1978 paper called "The Socialization of the Adopted Child" by Susan Laning, who is described as a "college-age adopted Asian daughter." It examines many aspects of transracial adoption and is available from International Concerns for Children in Boulder, Colorado.

Latin America and the Caribbean, India, the Philippines, many Asian countries, and since 1990, countries that once made up the former Soviet Union and other Eastern bloc nations. There are also limited opportunities to adopt from Africa.

Large-scale adoptions from China began around 1992 and spiraled upward as it became clear that there were many babies— mostly girls—who needed homes, and that the process was neither very difficult nor as expensive as other foreign adoptions, and completely legal. Furthermore, the Chinese government welcomed older parents and single adopters. What once seemed beyond reach for many aspiring parents was now available. Vibrant support networks grew in their wake.

Adoption has also become a big business. Go to any adoption conference for the first time, and you'll be surprised by the numbers of "advertisers"—agencies, facilitators, magazine publishers, insurance companies, greeting card vendors, and toy manufacturers—seeking to sell you their services. Talk to more experienced people in the field, and you'll learn that many newcomers are peddling services that they are not really equipped to provide. An experienced adoption expert I know bemoans the way one of her newer competitors "tries to tell people what they want to hear" to get them to sign on with her, rather than sketch out the realities of international adoption: how much it costs, what has to be done, the problems they may encounter—and the fact that children adopted internationally come from deprived backgrounds, and, although some are well cared for, others are hardly the sunny-faced, rosy-cheeked, chubby, and gurgly picture-book babies that parents imagine taking home. Not at first, anyway: the nurturing and love parents give is key to helping children get that way.

But the competition is tough. People seeking to adopt often do so after many years of *not* having children, and they don't want to wait. Many excellent professionals can help. But a sad reality is that some unscrupulous individuals or groups are giving adoption a bad name, making promises they can't keep, offering babies whose actual orphan status may be uncertain, and asking exorbitant sums of money to help families get them.

Technology and Changing Political Dynamics Make Adoption a Global Village

Fortunately, you can get information about the good, bad, and ugly agencies and services right at your fingertips—if you can type and know how to use a modem. One of the biggest changes in making international adoptions succeed is the wealth of information that is now available to adoption "consumers" as well as professionals. The Internet and the World Wide Web, fax technology and videotapes make it possible to transmit information and images in record time and enable people like you and me to obtain information that was once hard and expensive to track down.

This development has been a real boon. Adoption "chat groups" enable people to share information about their experiences and to highlight good agencies that do what they say and criticize those that don't. I think that over time, technology will also help balance out the wildly skewed costs of adoption that agencies charge. Agencies are having to become more competitive and accountable now, because *we* have ways of finding out who's charging less for better service, or who's making promises but not delivering. And we're learning that it's okay to ask the hard questions. If one agency doesn't satisfy us, we can find another that will help. Chapter 2 discusses the use of technology to get information and the questions you should ask when looking for an agency.

The new technology means that information about children—photo listings and videotapes—can get to prospective parents much faster. This is the most important part.

A number of people I profiled for this book cited the value of E-mail forums in helping them make wise choices about their adoption and also in providing moral support during the difficult waiting period and in sharing post-adoption experiences.

• When Alice, a forty-four-year-old lawyer who is single, was doing research on adopting an older child from overseas, one of the agencies she sought information from sent her videotapes of children in a Russian orphanage who were awaiting placement. Each child made a brief presentation, some also singing songs or dancing or reading a poem. In one segment, while a little boy was speaking, she was charmed by the sight, in the background, of a seven-year-old girl who was softly whispering the answers to the questions the boy was being asked. Nadia's lips would move, and then the boy's. Then the girl had her turn. Intrigued, Alice asked to find out more about her. She ultimately signed up with the agency and got a referral to adopt the girl, whose Russian name, Nadia, she kept.[2]

• Patti and Pete selected the agency they used to help them adopt Vietnamese twin boys based on recommendations in an E-mail forum. They had investigated a number of agencies on their own but drew on the forum's references to make their final choice.

• Bethany and Karl's adoption of a little girl from India benefited in many ways from access to E-mail. Through an Indian culture "newsgroup," they linked up with an Indian family living in the United States, and the father in that family, who came from the city where they eventually adopted their daughter, accompanied Bethany to India to complete the adoption. He helped negotiate through some of the red tape they encountered, and she believes his assistance saved her time and aggravation. Also, during the long wait for her adoption to be approved, she drew solace and support from other waiting parents participating in an Indian adoption E-mail forum.

---

[2] This is actually not her real name; I have changed names in the book to protect confidentiality.

WHERE INTERNATIONAL ADOPTIONS TAKE PLACE[3]

	1985	1990	1995
ALL COUNTRIES	9286	7057	9679
EUROPE: total	91	262	2711
Romania		121	275
Russian Federation			1896
Other former U.S.S.R.			341
Other Europe	91	141	199
ASIA: total	6991	3779	5040
China (mainland)	16	29	2130
India	496	348	371
Korea	5694	2620	1666
Philippines	515	421	298
Thailand	28	100	53
Vietnam			318
Other Asia	242	261	204
AFRICA/OCEANIA	20	62	109
AMERICAS: total	2184	2954	1819
Mexico	137	112	83
Dominican Republic	47	58	15
Haiti	12	64	49
El Salvador	310	103	30
Guatemala	175	257	449
Honduras	181	197	28

[3] Source: *National Adoption Reports,* January/February 1996. 1995 data from the U.S. State Department were preliminary at the time this chart was prepared.

	1985	1990	1995
Brazil	242	228	146
Chile	206	302	90
Colombia	622	631	350
Paraguay	15	282	351
Peru	34	440	15
Other Americas	203	280	213

Why People Adopt Internationally—and Why You Might Want To, Too

There are many reasons people seek children outside the United States, especially if they want relatively healthy infant children. Here are a few:

• **Too difficult to adopt in the United States.** For couples or single people seeking healthy newborns, there are not enough born in the United States who will be placed for adoption. Some single people who have tried to adopt United States–born children have encountered obstacles when they find themselves "competing" with couples. They then turn to international adoption because it is less bureaucratic and often faster to do.

• **Too "competitive."** Some people cannot stomach the prospect of "advertising" and having to be "selected" by a birth mother as the best possible parent for her child—and then perhaps face the prospect of this adoption falling through. (They even buy adoption insurance policies in the event they spend money to help a birth mother through her birth and she then decides to keep the child or choose a different family.) Two couples I know—Nanette and Rob, and Ava and Bob—found the idea of advertising themselves as ideal parents and setting up a toll-free number in their home to field calls from birth mothers to be utterly distasteful.

• **Too slow.** A domestic adoption can take well over a year to achieve. But if you're very organized and focused, you can complete an international adoption much more quickly.

Once they made their decision to adopt internationally and found the right resources to help them, it took Nanette and Rob just six months from their first filings to adopt their seven-month-old daughter from Guatemala.

• **Too expensive.** Yes, it can be more expensive to adopt domestically than to go overseas. To complete a legal domestic adoption for a newborn infant generally requires the intervention of a lawyer and the payment of the birth mother's hospital fees and occasional aftercare. The costs can be quite high.

• **Intrigued by the challenge of bringing a child from another culture into their lives.** I like this reason the best, and I saved the best for last. International adoption is a positive, reasonable, and wonderful way to form your family. Some people adopt internationally because they *want* their family experience to be a multicultural one. This could be because the family itself is "mixed," because the community they live in is a diverse, interesting one, or because one or both parents had lived abroad or it was where the family's roots came from. Once I began considering international adoption, and then when I actually started the process, I realized it was a gift—to me.

More People—and Different Types!—Are Doing International Adoptions

The criteria for international adoption in many countries has loosened up in the last decade. If you read Elizabeth Bartholet's excellent book *Family Bonds: Adoption and the Politics of Parenting,* you will be surprised at how much has changed since she undertook two adoptions in Peru in the mid-eighties. When she started out, single women, especially if they were over forty, as she was, were frowned upon as adoption candidates and discouraged.

These days, many first-time adopters are, in fact, single women in their forties. And many more countries are accepting single parents who have responsible jobs, are emotionally mature and stable, can show that they have a support system in place for the child, and are prepared to provide a loving home. While some countries still place children with couples only, or with families of a certain religion, many restrictions are slowly going by the wayside as more children need homes.

Generally, you may be considered a good candidate for adoption if you or your partner (if you have one) are a U.S. citizen, are at least twenty-five years old, have received home-study approval (which indicates you are emotionally and financially prepared to adopt), Immigration and Naturalization Service (INS) approval (which includes the home study, references, fingerprints, FBI check), child abuse clearance, and medical clearance (doctor's letter).

Few Boundaries: If You Have Always Wanted to Have a Family, Now You Can

Once you decide to do an international adoption and have ascertained that you have the resources to do it—and this takes time and serious thought—you will be gratified at the amount of support you will find.

I've benefited from the experiences of so many other people, and I'm sharing mine (and many of theirs) with you to let you know how to make your international adoption work for you.

2

Getting Started

I remember how intimidated I felt when I first sought information on how to do an international adoption. So I've put together this chapter to help you

1. Get good information.
2. Select the country that's right for you.
3. Choose whether an agency or facilitator is the route for you.

1. GETTING GOOD INFORMATION

When you embarked on your adoption, you probably started by telling your closest friends and relatives, by visiting a library or bookstore, or scanning the telephone book for listings under adoption. There's plenty of information to be had!

Much of it is free. But the nitty-gritty information on legal issues as well as different country requirements and, sometimes, requirements in the state you live in, may change without your knowing. Furthermore, not all the information you get may be good information. And new resources for people seeking to adopt, and for your adopted children, reach the market all the time.

Here are some of my recommendations to enable you to keep up to date and informed:

• **Read!** There are many magazines and newsletters on adoption that can introduce you to the world of adoption and the issues that accompany it. Here are a few that I recommend (see Appendix for the addresses and contact numbers for these publications): *Adoptive Families* magazine is my personal favorite. The magazine does a wonderful job of covering just about every aspect of doing an adoption and raising a family formed through adoption, as well as legislative issues. It lists upcoming conferences, cultural events, and "culture camps" around the United States. There's also a listing of pen pals for your children. And each issue includes articles divided into age groups on the milestones and issues adopted children sometimes confront as they grow up. Plus, you can learn about companies that offer products—books, toys, music, greeting cards—made especially for adoptive families. I also regularly read *AdopTalk*, the newsletter of my local chapter of the Adoptive Parents Committee (APC) and *Families with Children from China* newsletter, an invaluable source of information on adoption issues related to raising a child born in China, which also lists cultural and recreational family events and names of local families with whom to network. (See Appendix for a listing of newsletters for other types of international adoptions.)

For highly targeted information, the National Adoption Information Clearinghouse (NAIC) will send you a free *publications and services catalog* of fact sheets and brochures on adoption, including a number specifically on international adoption. Its *general adoption resources* fact sheet lists the addresses of INS district offices; national and regional organizations concerned with adoption broken down into categories such as advocacy and public policy, financial assistance, support networks, etc. It can also provide lists of support groups in your state.

• **Speak to people who have already completed foreign adoptions.** Find out why and how they did their adoption. Be candid with your questions. If money is an issue with you, ask how much they spent and how they were able to afford it. Some people may find this intrusive, so you will have to "scope out" those whom you think would be willing to speak with you about it.

An international adoption can be expensive, but there are ways to reduce the costs if you ask around, and people in the adoption "network" should be able to come up with good suggestions. One of the best pieces of advice that I received early on was this: *Don't see a lawyer!* In international adoption, a reputable agency should be able to do all the key work that is necessary, and *you* can do many of the other tasks yourself, with little difficulty—often by mail—such as obtaining and filling in your INS forms, completing your child's readoption, and arranging for your child's naturalization. (This book will also tell you how.) A lawyer's services would incur unnecessary fees.

• **Go to adoption seminars and conferences.** Adoption agencies, community colleges, YM/YWCAs, churches and synagogues, and other organizations often sponsor free or low-cost seminars to introduce the adoption process. The people leading the seminars are often adoption professionals who offer free sessions as a way to market their services. This is your opportunity to ask any questions you might have. Once you start hearing the same answers over and over again, you'll know you're ready to move.

• **Go on-line.** If you don't have a personal computer and don't plan to get one, this tip won't apply to you. But so many people I spoke to have benefited from adoption information that they obtained on-line that you might want to consider it, too. The bulletin boards are divided into topics—Romanian adoption, children with special needs, single parenting, etc.—that enable you to exchange information with parents sharing your concerns. On America Online, the service that I use, adoption "conferences" are held several times a week, and you can subscribe to the list announcing the times and topics. Then you just log on at the scheduled time (or during the time period) and participate. (Proper "netiquette" means that you stick to the topic, of course.)

Whether or not you subscribe to a commercial on-line service, you can also get tons of information on the World Wide Web. Many adoption agencies and support groups have Web pages that provide information (including fees and photo listings) and details on how to adopt. (See also "The Technology Revolution," below, and Appendix, pages 166–69.)

• **Contact as many agencies and adoption organizations as you feel you need to.** Use recommendations from people who have *recently* had a successful experience with the agency or agencies to get started. This is important, because a particularly good agency program might be the result of one individual who built it up. If that person has gone elsewhere, the agency may no longer have good contacts in the country you may wish to adopt from. You will be surprised at the range of services and costs that agencies provide. Alice, a lawyer who describes herself as a compulsive researcher, wrote to twenty-five agencies when she got started. She adopted an eight-year-old girl from Russia; her story is in Chapter 9.

• **Don't be shy about asking questions of the agencies, especially regarding costs, timetables, and the services they provide.** Don't feel embarrassed about calling them again for new information or just to review some of the information they have already given you. A sign of a good agency is its responsiveness to your requests, the thoroughness of what you are told, and the consistency of information from whomever you speak to at the agency. (See discussion below on selecting a facilitator or agency.)

• **Find out if the state you live in has special requirements regarding international adoptions or working with INS.** Some states require you to have an agency do your home study while others accept home studies done by licensed, approved social workers. Contact a local adoption agency or referral service for information, or the attorney general's office in your state. *If you move to another state before your adoption is complete, you may have to file new documents.*

• **Be organized.** My three basic pointers on tracking an adoption are:

1. Start a file.
2. Order duplicates or make file copies of any documents or papers needed.
3. Keep a log of phone calls/conversations.

Doing any type of adoption requires a great deal of paperwork. And sometimes, unexpectedly, you have to produce a new batch of paperwork. As soon as you get started, create an "Adoption" file. You can subdivide your files as they get bigger: letters of reference (with duplicates), birth certificates, financial statements, copies of your home study, key correspondence, an INS file, copies of checks or receipts, and so on.

You can send photocopies of some documents to your agency or INS and keep the originals for yourself—but check this out first. It sometimes helps to get duplicate documents for your files. I ordered four copies of my birth certificate from the Vital Records Division of the New York City Department of Health, and although I didn't need all four, I was glad I had them. I also had two extra fingerprint cards for my file. If you have pictures of yourself taken for your visa, take two extras. You never know when they might come in handy, and you may want to take them with you when you travel.

2. CHOOSING WHERE TO ADOPT

Once you have decided to adopt internationally, you will want to decide which country or countries to consider. This choice is important, because once you have made it, you will be able to make a clearer choice on how to move forward with your adoption.

Here are some concerns to help you decide:

• **Your own background and comfort level.** I've run into on-line "chats" in which some people discussed their concern about adopting a child from a different ethnic background from theirs. If you feel any reservations about ethnic or racial differences, don't be afraid to express them. It could interfere with your ability to bond with your child. You might discover that whether or not your child resembles you doesn't matter as much as you thought—or that it matters very much. The needs and experiences of my own friends who have adopted children differ widely. Patti and Peter (see below, "The Technology Revolution") were initially intent on adopting a child from Eastern Europe (Patti's roots are Polish), but decided to take a very different route (first Korea, then Vietnam) when they realized that they would have a child much quicker—and far younger—by doing so. Their decision required intense soul-searching: they were concerned about racial differences and the difficulties their child might encounter. But their discussions with other adoptive parents as well as their own worldview—they have lived in Africa and South America and have traveled widely—made them feel better prepared.

• **Your affinity for a particular culture.** Ava and Bob chose to adopt a Russian child because they had lived and worked in

Russia for a number of years and felt very close to the Russian people and culture. They also spoke Russian fluently. Carol, whose husband is a rabbi, adopted her daughter from China because she had lived and worked there and felt a particularly affinity for Chinese people; she also had the necessary contacts to make the adoption proceed relatively smoothly.

• **Your community.** Do you feel that the community you live in would be a comfortable place for a child from a different background? My impression is that many urban areas, particularly, have become so diverse—and family structures are changing so much—that it is nowhere as difficult to be an interracial/intercultural family as it used to be. University towns are also often easier for mixed families, because they have many foreign students and sometimes also have cultural activities that might fit in with your child's background.

Alice, the lawyer I mentioned earlier, lives in such a town in Florida. She found a Russian tutor to give her private lessons before she went off to Russia herself to complete her adoption, and credits her ability to speak Russian with making a huge difference with her new daughter. Judi Kloper says that her family's proximity to a university in Oregon has made it easier for her mixed household (three children born in India, one in China, and one in the United States) to blend in well with the community. I've known of families that moved away from all-white suburbs to mixed communities in order to ensure that their children (and they) would feel more comfortable.

Some families that do not live in such mixed communities see their international adoption as an opportunity to create a greater sense of diversity. Bethany and Karl live in a resort town in Wisconsin, where they have two birth sons and their adopted daughter from India, Adina. Bethany describes herself as tall and blond and notes that her husband and children are also blond and big-boned. Adina, however, is small-boned and quite dark-skinned. Bethany had always wanted a daughter and was intrigued by the opportunity to adopt in India. She has felt that the adoption has very much enriched her family because of the exposure to Indian culture. The family prepared for the adoption for a long time and made sure that their sons' friends and families, as well as their neighbors, were aware of it long before it happened. They have been generally supportive.

• **Availability of support groups.** You might find out if there are organizations in your community that specialize in the culture of your child's birth country or on raising a "transcultural" family. Or else, you might want to start a support group yourself! (Many Chinese adoptions have taken place in my own neighborhood, and my membership in the Families with Children from China network has been invaluable for me, both as a single mother and a first-time parent.)

• **Your gut feeling.** You will be the parent, so ultimately the decision has to be based on what you feel in your heart and gut about the type of child you will believe you can truly love.

Some resources that may help you decide include:

• *Adoptive Families* magazine and other publications and books that frequently address these issues. (See resources in Appendix.)

• **On-line bulletin boards.** Some of these focus specifically on cultural issues, which you can discuss with other parents around the country who have gone through—or are now going through—what you're experiencing.

Some people adopt from countries where their families originally came from because of similar ethnic roots. Others adopt from countries they may have lived or work in and for which they feel an affinity. Be true to yourself, and don't let other people try to tell you what you *should* do based on what *they* think. After all, this is *your* child and *your* family—and *your* decision!

3. HOW TO GO ABOUT IT:
AGENCY, FACILITATOR, OR INDEPENDENT?

In the course of your adoption research and networking, you will hear about many different ways that people have adopted. I subscribe to the "whatever works" theory, namely, find what works for you, *but make sure that your choice is based on solid research and references.* You should not enter into a project or a "relationship" with an agency unless you feel that your questions have been answered and that you feel confident. Similarly, although you may hear glowing reports about a particular facilitator, you should go beyond that facilitator's own referrals and even those of an individual who recommends the person and do a background check with INS and other resources (such as your local APC chapter) that might be able to fill you in.

The Agency Option

A good agency offers a complete infrastructure with experts who will guide you through every step of the way and provide backup in case of problems. The agency should have a track record of relatively prompt placements from the country from which you are adopting, and be able to communicate its services clearly and provide recent references. Agencies vary in their services, skills, and capacity. New ones are being started all the time, often by people who have had successful experiences in adopting and want to help others to do so. Some established agencies may have good programs in some countries but weak programs in others.

You must get references and talk to other people who have used the agency. Look *beyond* the agency for these references. Your local adoption support organization and on-line forums can be very helpful this way. (Make sure the agency is licensed.)

A good agency should do the following:

- Respond to your questions honestly, promptly, and completely
- Provide you with a comprehensive list of its services and its fees for those services
- Inform you of additional fees you may be required to pay, including, for instance, estimated travel costs and expenses you may encounter to complete the adoption that are not covered by the agency
- Not make you pay up front for an adoption, but rather seek the fees when a referral comes through and you agree to accept it (a nonrefundable application fee of $150 or $200 is usually requested to get the process going)
- Have a backup plan if something should happen in the country, such as a program in another country that suits you, and a priority placement for you if you have been waiting for a long time; or offer the option of a refund if the placement you were hoping for falls through and you decide to withdraw from that agency
- Keep you informed of any changes
- Be helpful and supportive if delays occur in the adoption that are not in the agency's control
- Offer postplacement support
- Provide a payment plan if you are unable to pay your total fees at one time

Judi Kloper, who has worked with agencies in Oregon, suggests also that a good agency should:

- Give adequate and accurate answers to your questions
- Make sure that all employees have the same information
- Give you a step-by-step checklist of the things *you* need to do to complete your dossier
- Give you a complete itinerary of your trip, if you travel

- Tell you how many placements it has made in the country you wish to adopt from, and when these took place
- Have a special program if you are interested in adopting a special-needs child
- Accommodate you or your partner if one is disabled
- Have not-for-profit[1] status

Avoid agencies, she adds, that

- Have a religious slant that you are not comfortable with or which might work against your application
- Bad-mouth other agencies (a bad sign)
- Demand high fees up front with no accounting on how the money is being used
- Treat you like a nuisance when you ask for progress on your application

Patti and Pete, who adopted twin boys from Vietnam, used an agency that had already placed more than sixty Vietnamese children with families and had good relationships with several excellent orphanages. Pete, who has traveled extensively for his work, noted that the children at the orphanage did not cling to visitors in the fashion that he had seen elsewhere, which was, he said, a sign that the children were well cared for and got a lot of individual attention. Despite some glitches during their trip (such as the fact that their translator didn't really understand English, although she always nodded and said, "Yes, yes"!), their placement went relatively smoothly. They had the opportunity to see the orphanage where their sons were staying and gained custody of their sons the day after they arrived in Saigon. They stayed in Vietnam for just two weeks. While they were there,

---

[1] I have heard an opposing opinion on this; whether an agency is for-profit or not-for-profit does not necessarily mean that one is better than the other if, for instance, the not-for-profit agency is paying a few staff hefty salaries.

they met a man who was adopting a child through another agency that had fewer contacts and had made fewer placements. He stayed in Vietnam for almost two months. A third man they met, who was adopting two children, had had to make two separate trips to complete the adoption and take them home. Some disadvantages of agencies:

• They may be expensive.
• They may have a long waiting list for the country you want to adopt from.
• They may seem impersonal.
• If you are working with an agency from out of state, you may rack up high telephone and fax bills, though some agencies now have toll-free numbers.
• Agencies vary widely in their competence and contacts. Unless you do a thorough check of the one you choose to work with, you could end up making a costly and time-consuming error of affiliating with an agency that has lost its accreditation, makes promises it can't keep, or takes money from you without delivering a service.

The bottom line is that the agency search is ultimately up to you. There are lots of agencies out there, and you need to do your homework. Get references, either through your local support organization or through an on-line service. **Don't be afraid to ask questions—and don't do anything that you don't feel absolutely comfortable with!**

My choice: I used an agency that was highly recommended to me by the woman who did my home study. I had a list of names of people, including single mothers who lived in my neighborhood, who had completed their adoptions through that agency, and they gave it glowing reviews. I was also impressed by the relatively low fees the agency charged and the fact that I was required to pay nothing more than a nominal application fee until my referral came through and I signed a contract agreeing to the referral. Throughout my dealings within this agency, I found its staff to be prompt and responsive to my queries.

The Facilitator Option

A facilitator may be a lawyer or a layperson with contacts in a foreign country and can help link you to authorities in that country able to identify an infant or a very young child who is legally available for adoption. Many facilitators are actually from the country and/or have relatives there who have contacts with orphanages and/or government agencies. The advantage of a good facilitator is that you can save time by breaking through red tape, and, sometimes, money.

At one time, facilitators marketed themselves as a lower-cost alternative to agencies. These days, I am hearing quotes of facilitator fees that are as high as agency fees—and sometimes even higher—but without the same services. What I believe to be the case is that facilitators market themselves as able to help arrange placements faster and, sometimes, to households that might not normally qualify under certain agency requirements. **Get references if you are thinking of using a facilitator!** These days, the difference between an agency and a facilitator is not very great. As one adoption professional put it, an agency is actually a facilitator, too, but with more infrastructure.

Advantages of a good facilitator:

- Can save time
- Can work with you more directly
- May be less expensive than an agency
- May have more direct contacts
- May be a more efficient option for you if you have country contacts yourself and need an intermediary in that country to make access easier, particularly if there's a language barrier

- May work with you if an agency will not, such as if you're older than the average accepted candidate for adoption

Disadvantages of a facilitator:

- Little or none of the infrastructure a good agency provides
- Sometimes informal or unavailable
- Often no contract, no guarantees, minimal accountability
- Not always as professional or reliable as a good agency
- Information may not be current or thorough
- Often no follow-through when the adoption is completed

Three facilitator stories:

I. Through a friend in her synagogue with two adopted children from Paraguay, Irene was put in contact with a facilitator who promised to help her with an adoption. At forty-eight, Irene did not want to wait long; she had already spent many years considering adoption and assessing her situation, and now that she had made up her mind, she didn't want to find herself in the position of waiting until no one would help her any longer. She also was no longer a candidate for many agencies because of her age.

The facilitator, whom we'll call Anna, lived elsewhere but happened to be visiting the city where Irene lives. Their meeting was delightful. She charged Irene $3,000 for her service, which was to act as an intermediary between Irene and a lawyer in Asunción who could identify children available for adoption. An assignment came through for just the type of child Irene had dreamed of raising: a beautiful eighteen-month-old girl. Irene was then put in touch with the lawyer, who charged $15,000 to move the adoption through the Paraguayan legal system. Irene would need to go to Paraguay twice: first, to file court papers for the adoption and to undergo a psychological test. She also met her daughter and spent time with her. (Irene bought many beautiful new outfits for her daughter to wear during the visit, but on the facilitator's advice, she took the clothes back home with her.) The second trip would come after the papers had been processed and approved, and Irene would be allowed to take her daughter home.

But then things stumbled. The translator in Asunción lost her papers not once, but twice. Irene was frantic, although each time the papers were found within days. Also, her interactions with the Paraguayan consulate were often unpleasant. She was made to pay extra fees each time she had to file papers and had the feeling that some of the fees were not required. In any case, she had not been told about these fees and blames the facilitator. "After I paid my money, she would never return calls, and was often rude, telling me not to call so early or so late," Irene complained. But Irene teaches school and was unable to make calls during regular office hours. Irene, who is single, felt lonely, isolated, and angry during this time, but she had no recourse. For one thing, she had already paid thousands of dollars to the facilitator and the lawyer. For another, she was afraid that if she said anything to alienate Anna, Anna might possibly become vindictive and not help her out or at least stall. Even without the support of an agency, Irene ended up spending about $23,000 for her adoption, including the two trips to Paraguay. Furthermore, Irene learned that the friend who had hooked her up to Anna had received a commission for the referral. This knowledge upset her, since she realized that there was more than mere friendly interest in providing help.

Irene's story has a happy ending: her adoption ultimately came through and she is thrilled to have an energetic and healthy daughter who quickly became attached to her new mother, her new home, and her many new friends. But Irene is still bitter about the experience.

II. Nicole chose to use a facilitator to help her adopt a Chinese infant girl. Nicole could have gone with an agency, as there were many of them in her area with China programs, but she chose instead to use the services of a Chinese woman she had met at a meeting in New York City of Families with Children from China. She had several reasons. In the first place, the facilitator was willing to help Nicole for a low fee, because this would be one of the first placements she had done and she wanted to see how smoothly it would go. In the second place, Nicole, who is a freelance writer, wanted to save money and was willing to do a lot of the legwork that an agency often does. And, furthermore, she happens to be quite independent and was willing to take the risk.

There was one hitch in the process. Soon after her paperwork was done, Nicole got a distressing piece of news: two referrals had come through and Nicole had to choose one! How to do this? Photographs of infant girls had been faxed from China to the facilitator and Nicole had to look at them and, on that basis, decide which would become her daughter for life. This was a hellish dilemma. She chose the first one, feeling a bond that she could not quite describe. But she did not feel fully at peace with her choice.

Ultimately, when Nicole went to China, she not only picked up her new daughter, but traveled to the other orphanage in another city many hours away to see the child she was not taking. "I had to do this," says Nicole. And although she found the voyage fascinating, it is a situation she wishes she didn't have to experience—and it should not happen to you.

III. David and Donna had a terrible experience with one facilitator and an excellent one with another. The difference seems to be that in the first case, they were inexperienced with the process and didn't ask the right questions. They were too trusting when they should not have been. In the second, they made sure to check the references of their facilitator thoroughly.

In the first case, David and Donna undertook an adoption in Lithuania and were required by their facilitator to pay an upfront fee of $15,000. A child was assigned to them, but then the laws in Lithuania changed, requiring that orphanages seek Lithuanian families first before placing children outside of the country. A family was found for the child designated for them, and they were unable to reclaim any of the $15,000 they had spent.

They then did a very thorough search for references to help them adopt elsewhere in Eastern Europe. They were referred to an adoption lawyer who places many Russian children with U.S. families, and was even able to do so in 1995 when Russian adoptions were placed on hold. To check his credentials, David and Donna called their local INS office, and the attorney received "flying colors," they said. This attorney has established a charitable foundation to facilitate adoptions, and $1,000 of his fees go to the foundation and are therefore tax-deductible. Also, he requires a relatively low sum of money up front to move the process along—about $3,000 of the $6,500 necessary to adopt a child who is at least five years old. All fees are placed into a trust, and clients receive monthly statements of where the money has gone until a referral comes through and the parents accept it. At that time, the parents pay the balance.

This attorney has a full-time employee in St. Petersburg who handles much of the bureaucratic paperwork in Russia on behalf of parents (they sign a power of attorney to this individual), thus minimizing the amount of travel and the time they must be in the country. In fact, just one trip is required and only one parent must go to Russia, which is not always the case.

The Independent Option

Some people choose to adopt on their own. As a result of travels or work in a foreign country, or by virtue of their origin from a country where adoptions take place, they may know of a child who needs a home and have the contacts to make the adoption possible. This is generally an exceptional situation and requires a certain personality type and persistence to see it through as well as "pedigree" contacts. The Bureau of Consular Affairs in the U.S. State Department can provide you with the information you need to do such an adoption (see page 40).

The advantage is that you are in charge of the process, and if you are a "control freak," as one man who did such an adoption from China described himself, then this is the way for you to go. It can be done—no one will hold your hand—and you will save agency fees, sometimes thousands of dollars. It helps to be absolutely determined and to have a strong stomach!

I know of a few such cases: Theresa, who has many relatives in the Dominican Republic, adopted her first son using family contacts there to link up with a reputable adoption attorney, who served as an intermediary between her and a local orphanage that was able to identify an infant boy waiting for permanent placement with a loving family.

Eileen and Jerry adopted their two Romanian children using a local facilitator. The first time was in 1990, just when Romania had opened for adoption and agencies had not yet established footholds there. The second time, in 1993, was when the biological mother of their daughter gave birth to a son that she knew she could not keep. She contacted the facilitator who had aided the first adoption, and the facilitator contacted Eileen and Jerry. At that time, Romanian adoptions were only supposed to take place through accredited agencies, and Eileen and Jerry therefore signed up with an agency that promised to help them. When they learned that the son was ill and languishing in an orphanage, they prodded the agency to move with their application.

The agency seemed to be dragging its feet. "We were worried that our son might not make it," says Eileen. So she and Jerry took a risky step. They went to Romania themselves, and, with the help of their facilitator (and the experience of their first adoption), managed to move the adoption through the proper channels so they could take their son home. Their son had many physical problems that were not looked after in the orphanage but that his parents took care of immediately on their return. "He might have died if we hadn't brought him home," Jerry says. They refused to pay their agency, and consider this to have been an independent adoption.

Patti and Pete—the adoptive parents of Vietnamese twins whom I mentioned earlier—described a friend with government contacts in Vietnam, where he had worked, and how he tried to use them to pursue an independent adoption. The adoption went through, but the man didn't save money. He ultimately had to pay plenty of fees to "bribe" the government contacts so that the paperwork would be approved. The friend strongly discouraged Patti and Pete from this method!

I have recently read that independent adoptions are being discouraged by authorities in China. I would surmise that this has to do with the huge increase in families seeking to adopt there, and that the authorities find it easier to work with agencies that have several families adopting in a group. If you wish to adopt in this manner, be sure to find out how feasible this is in the country in which you adopt. I learned this information from a couple that had done two independent adoptions in China. They were advising new parents not to do it.

THE TECHNOLOGY REVOLUTION

When I started preparing this book in late 1995, I was a novice to the world of on-line services. Over time I became an avid user of electronic mail (E-mail) and was able to get tons of information without ever leaving my home—and my computer.

Taking advantage of adoption "chat lines" and newsgroups, I came into contact with networks of people and organizations that answered many of my questions—and allayed many of my anxieties—without having to spend more than the rather nominal fee I was paying for my service. (Depending on your subscription arrangement, you may pay between $10 to $25—or more—per month to go on-line.)

Many of my interview contacts for this book were made through America Online's adoption network. I reached people as far afield as Oregon, Wisconsin, Florida, Indiana, Massachusetts, California, Pennsylvania, and Virginia—and could have gone much farther if I had wanted to or needed to. I also discovered contacts close to home, and met a number of families in person as a result. *Many* people I interviewed said that their participation on-line had made a critical difference in their choices of agencies and in helping them to avoid key mistakes.

"Whenever I had a question about anything in Vietnam, including my agency, I put it on-line," says Patti, whom I mentioned earlier. She had hoped to adopt from Eastern Europe because "I always wanted a blue-eyed Caucasian child," then considered Korea because she and Pete wanted an infant soon and didn't want to wait as long as Eastern European adoptions were taking. On the on-line Korean discussion forum, Patti learned that many baby boys were available for placement. After contacting fifteen agencies, Patti felt frustrated "because it was hard to get straight answers" and once again drew on on-line resources to select the agency she and Pete finally used to adopt in Vietnam. "Everyone on-line said for us to go with this agency," Patti says. Indeed, a referral came through four months after their documentation was finished, and she and Peter had twin sons just three months later. On-line discussions helped even more when Patti was getting ready to travel. It was January, "so we prepared to take diapers and winter clothes for babies," Patti says. But disposable diapers were available in Saigon, they were advised, and it would be very hot. Leave the heavy clothes at home, said their on-line contacts, and they did.

Bethany and Karl's year-long wait to travel to India to get their daughter, Adina, was made less painful through the immense support she received from other parents whom she met on-line who had either completed adoptions in India or were also waiting for the go-ahead to travel to the same orphanage in Hyderabad. As a result of the contacts she made, she arranged to have other traveling parents bring gifts to her child and to take photographs of her. In addition, through her participation on an Indian culture on-line newsgroup, her family, which lives in Wisconsin, befriended an Indian family living in Missouri, who were originally from Hyderabad. In fact, the father in that family accompanied Bethany to India and helped her wade through some of the bureaucracy she encountered. She and he are now considering forming an agency of their own to facilitate adoptions in Hyderabad.

Many agencies now have Web pages on the Internet. You can find many of them using a Web browser and the key word "Adoption Agency." Agencies and adoption organizations are increasingly including their Web page addresses in their advertising information. The Web pages are excellent resources, and if you print them out you can do comparative shopping of the different services agencies offer and their prices.

The on-line adoption center also has bulletin boards on adoptive parenting so that if you ever notice anything about your child that makes you anxious (aside from an obvious medical question), or anything about the process, you can post it on the board. You are likely to get numerous responses. I experienced this myself when I posted the news of my referral, the agency I was working with, and my concern about a delay in my expected travel date. I remain active on-line as an adoptive mom.

When you consider how much there is to do, you will ultimately save money and time by taking advantage of the technology option, provided that you already have a computer. And if you don't, here's the perfect excuse to buy one. Most computers these days come with high speed modems and free access to on-line services. You can get a home computer with a high-speed modem for under $1,800.

Fax technology, which I learned about on-line, also plays a role in getting adoption information. The U.S. State Department and INS will fax through to you thorough guidelines on international adoption plus specific country information if you have a fax machine that has its own receiver. You can buy such a fax machine for under $200. (See Chapter 3 on working with INS.)

3

The Next Steps

Once you have decided where you are going to adopt and how you will do it, you have a number of tasks ahead that only you can do. These include

1. Opening an adoption file with the U.S. Immigration and Naturalization Service
2. Scheduling a home study
3. Collecting documents for your dossier

Once these tasks are done, the next two steps involve *waiting* and *waiting: waiting* for a referral—which *will* come through, even if at times you stop believing, and then *waiting* again— sometimes not for very long but sometimes for longer than you'd like—to get your child, either by traveling to your child's birth country or through an escort arrangement in which your child is brought to you.

Paperwork??? Paperwork!!!

There's just no avoiding it. Completing an adoption means collecting lots of papers. Some adoptive parents compare phases of the adoption to the phases of pregnancy. Many of the anxieties are no doubt similar. The early stage of making the decision and doing the paperwork felt like morning sickness. (I often wondered if I'd go through with it, and I sometimes felt queasy.) But the day my INS approval arrived, I felt like I'd gotten a positive pregnancy test, and the announcement of my referral made me think I might be going into labor.

But, seriously, if you're an organized person to begin with, it will work out. I frankly became much more organized as I proceeded with the adoption, and I think this will help me as a parent since I will have to keep much better track of my finances for tax, insurance, education, and medical purposes.

If you make an organized list of what you will actually need, the paperwork isn't as difficult as you might think.

Here is a basic checklist of the tasks you must do:

Open your INS file.
Schedule the home study.
File for child abuse clearance.
Collect documentation that will be required for the home-
   study file and the country where you will be adopting.

OPEN YOUR INS FILE

There are two possible forms to file. If you have identified an available child, you will file the blue form I-600: Petition to Classify Orphan as an Immediate Relative. If this is what you are doing, you will need to collect a lot more information about the child, such as proof of age, death certificate of parent(s), if applicable, and assorted documentation that proves beyond question that the child has been abandoned. Of course, you will also need a home study and need to follow the other procedures that all adoptive parents must follow when seeking to adopt overseas.

But most of you won't have a specific child in mind yet, and you're the ones I'm writing for. So you will need to file the orange form I-600A to get the process started. This is called the Application for Advance Processing of Orphan Petition and indicates that you wish to adopt and want to get the paperwork in place so that when you go overseas (often under the auspices of an agency or facilitator) the paperwork will be ready to complete the adoption. Pending your approval to adopt, these forms are sent both to the National Visa Center and to the consulate of the country where you will be adopting. (Parents who originally file the I-600A will then file the I-600 at the country consulate when the adoption is completed. The form will be at the consulate.) When you request the I-600A, you will also get the I-600. Keep it in your files.

File the initial forms right away. INS needs to do an FBI check of your background which, depending on where you live, can take a few weeks or a few months. With the I-600A, you do *not* have to know from which country you are adopting; you don't even have to have chosen how to do it, that is, with an agency, facilitator, or on your own. Fill in what you do know or what you *think* you'll be doing. You may make changes.

At this writing, the I-600A costs $155 and is good for eighteen months. So is your home study. But if you send it to INS more than six months after you filed your I-600A, you will have to do an update. This was my case.

The Bureau of Consular Affairs at the U.S. Department of State publishes an excellent twenty-three-page guide entitled *International Adoptions* (Department of State 10300). It tells you in plain English everything you need to know on working with

INS and completing an international adoption. In addition, the Office of Children's Issues has some country-specific information and also provides the names of some support groups. To get the guide, write to: Office of Children's Issues, CA/OCS/CI, Room 4811, Department of State, Washington, DC 20520–4818; phone: (202)647-2688; fax: (202)647-2835.

There's also a twenty-four-hour line at (202)736-7000 with recorded telephone messages with information on specific countries. If you want flyers with information about specific countries, you can send an 8½-by-11-inch stamped, self-addressed envelope to OCS.

If you have a fax machine with its own telephone receiver, you can obtain the guide instantly by phoning (202)647-3000. You will hear a recording instructing how to order a series of documents. Make your call on a Sunday or when your long-distance rates are lowest because of the numbers of pages and time involved. Some of the country-specific information is quite long.

INS publishes a booklet entitled *The Immigration of Adopted and Prospective Adoptive Children* that details specific immigration requirements. You can obtain it by calling your local INS office or order it from a toll-free information line at (800)755-0777. Ask for brochure M-249-Y.

The information you get includes a full description of the processes required to complete an international adoption, whether you do it independently or with an intermediary such as an agency or a facilitator.

There are also information packets on individual countries where adoptions are currently taking place. At the time I called, these included the following thirty-four countries:

Belarus, Belize, Bolivia, Brazil, Bulgaria, China, Colombia, Costa Rica, Czech Republic, Dominican Republic, Estonia, Georgia, Germany, Greece, Guatemala, Haiti, Ireland, Korea, Latvia, Mexico, Moldova, Nicaragua, Panama, Paraguay, Peru,

Philippines, Russia, Rwanda, Slovakia, Thailand, Ukraine, Uruguay, Uzbekistan, and Vietnam.

Part I: INS Preadoption Step-by-Step
1. Obtain I-600A from INS ($155 at this writing) and fill in as soon as possible.
2. Have sets of fingerprints made (I kept two extra cards for my file, just in case, although I didn't need them; $16 for the first two cards, $1 dollar more for each additional).
3. Make arrangements for a home study. Depending on where you live, this may either be through your agency or through an independent specialist—usually a social worker—who is licensed to do home studies.
4. Get copies of your birth or baptismal certificate.
5. Mail back to INS with fee, fingerprint cards, letters of reference, birth certificate, and completed home study. The home study is considered valid for six months from the time it is completed.
6. Wait.
7. Within a few weeks usually or a couple of months, you will receive Form I-171H from INS. This one-page document lets you know that your file petition has been approved and that your file has been sent or is being sent to the consulate in the country from which you wish to adopt. Your birth certificate and home study will be returned to you.

Part II: How to Work with INS/U.S. Consular Services After the Assignment Comes
1. You will make arrangements to travel to the country to pick up your child (or your agency will act on your behalf with a local contact and escort). In most cases, you will have your child within a day or two of arriving.

2. You (or an agency representative) will go to the U.S. consulate in that country to obtain a visa for your child ($200 at this writing).

3. This process will require a medical checkup for your child. Your agency should tell you the cost, as you will have to pay for it in cash. This can often be directly arranged through the consulate, or else the consulate will advise you on how to set up an appointment.

4. Take a few breaths . . . take lots of photographs . . . and look around you.

5. Then go home.

Part III: Your Child is Yours

1. A non-INS task may be the "readoption" of your child in your state court. This is not required in every state. Check with your agency and local social services office about it. A key advantage is that your child will be able to get a U.S. birth certificate.

2. Citizenship can be applied for at any time until your child reaches eighteen years old. Your child will need a Social Security card beforehand. You can get that at any time (after your child's Green Card arrives). It's better to do it sooner than later. (See Chapter 7 for information on applying for your child's citizenship and Social Security card.)

Pointers on Working with INS

In New York City, where I live, the image we have of INS is of frighteningly long lines of anxious foreigners applying for green cards. These lines form soon after midnight, snake many miles around the block, and people still often don't get the documents they want.

As adopting parents, you do *not* need to make a personal trip to INS. A phone call will suffice. In New York, there is a recorded message and I was able to leave my name and address and in a relatively short time I had the forms I needed. This could be different where you live depending on how busy the INS office is. And many of you may live a long distance away, so it is not feasible to make a personal visit without giving up time at work.

If you have problems contacting your local office, you can get the forms by contacting: INS Eastern Region Forms Center, 11 Elmwood Avenue, Burlington, VT 05401–4391; (800)755-0777

HINT: Request two copies of the I-600-A, just in case. And make copies of anything you send out for your own file.

Getting Fingerprints Made

You need not make a special trip to INS to have your fingerprints taken. I went to my local police precinct. However, a rookie cop with evidently little experience doing fingerprints made a mess of the two cards INS sent me. A senior officer then did my prints on precinct fingerprint cards, which are identical to the INS cards except that they have a typed-in code that indicated they were from the precinct. I was worried that these would not be acceptable to INS, so I called to find out. INS said they were okay.

Different INS offices may have their own requirements. If you have any questions, make sure to speak to your INS office first so you won't be disappointed later.

Getting Letters of Reference
for Your Application

I needed three letters. I chose people who know me well personally. I had met two of them initially as an employee, so they were able to provide both a professional and personal assessment. You can send photocopies. I've kept the originals in my file.

Optional Tasks

Apply for or renew your passport, as necessary, if you have to travel to get your child. This can be done by mail and usually takes less than three weeks from the time you send it in. Many large post offices and federal courthouses have passport offices. New application fee: $65; renewal fee: $55. For further information, call (800)688-9889.

SCHEDULE THE HOME STUDY

Checklist:

- Identify a person to do the home study (unless your state requires that you do the home study with an agency).
- Schedule the interview.
- Obtain a child abuse clearance.
- Undertake document collection:
  Birth certificate(s)
  Marriage license, if applicable
  Divorce and/or death certificates, if applicable (you may have to go to an out-of-state courthouse or county office to obtain these)
  Financial statements
    Recent pay stub
    Front page of your most recent 1040 tax return
    Accountant's letter or other documentation of investments and bank accounts
  Employer's letter to verify employment and salary; if self-employed, get an accountant's letter

Proof of home ownership and/or rent statement
Letters of reference
Physician's report (may have to be notarized)
Good conduct certificate

The Home Study

The home study is *not* a description of your home. It is a profile of the type of person you are and the type of emotionally supportive and financially stable home that you will provide for a child. It is not something to feel threatened about, unless you have a troubled background or are trying to hide something. And you do not have to be wealthy.

Basically, the home study aims to collect biographical information on the adoptive parent(s), their family backgrounds, why he/she/they are adopting, their personal and professional history, their feelings about raising children, their personal interests, and the qualities that make them potentially good parents. The home study is required no matter whether you work with an agency or a facilitator.

The living space you have for a child is examined as part of the study, but it is not the main feature of the home study.

You will normally need to provide some documentation for the home study to be completed. This is usually easy material to provide. It includes:

1. *Birth or baptismal certificate(s), and, if it applies, marriage and/or divorce decrees.* The health department or vital records unit in the city or county where you were born should have this documentation if you don't. I was able to order birth certificates by phone using a credit card. I say *certificates* because I made sure I had extras just in case. I also needed to get an "exemplified" birth certificate for China (one with an extra seal from the secretary of state of the applicant's state of residence) and was

able to request this by phone. I saved a lot of time, even though I had paid a $5 surcharge per certificate. It was worth it.

2. *Child abuse clearance with the state you live in.* You will be required to fill in a basic form answering a few background questions. It is a pro forma process that takes a few weeks to make its way through the state bureaucracy; it is painless (unless you're trying to hide something) and doesn't cost much (I paid $35). Your agency may do it for you if it's based in the state you live in; if you are working with a facilitator or an out-of-state agency, you can ask an authorized agency to do it for you. This was my case; the social worker who did my home study recommended an agency that did it. The agency sent me the forms and handled the subsequent paperwork. (If you are uncertain how to do this, contact your local adoption support group for advice.)

3. *Financial statements.* I provided a recent pay stub, photocopies of bank books to show my current savings, and an estimate of the amount of money I have invested in IRAs, CDs, and other accounts. (If asked, I can provide printed statements, but this has not been necessary.) For my update, I asked my bank to write a letter listing my accounts to date and their value.

4. *Proof of employment.* My employer wrote a letter stating my annual salary and how long I had been employed. If self-employed, you should get an accountant's letter.

5. *First page of the previous year's federal tax return (1040).* You should have a copy, otherwise check with your tax preparer.

6. *Letters of reference.* Three people. In my case, two of the letters were from people with whom I had worked.

7. *Document of home ownership or a rent statement.* I submitted a copy of the deed of ownership of my cooperative apartment.

You must do a home study for any adoption. The home study is destined both for your INS file and for the country from which you are adopting. The home study must be done by someone who is licensed in your state or by an agency if you live in an "agency state." If you have the choice, look for someone who has written home studies for the country you plan to adopt from and ask people you know to recommend a person with that experience. Each country has certain requirements and the experienced home-study writer will be familiar with different country concerns and also how to interpret you as an appropriate candidate for parenting a child from that country.

Feel free—feel *entitled*—to interview the person whom you may be hiring to do your home study. This individual will be asking for intimate details of your life, and you should feel absolutely comfortable with her or him. Some questions you might ask are:

How long have you been doing adoption home studies?

How many children have you helped to place?

(If not employed by an agency:) How many agencies are you connected with? Which ones are these? How long have you had these ties? (Then double-check with the agency/ies you are considering working with.)

Have you done many home studies for the country from which I wish to adopt?

What are your fees for the different services you offer? (These should be made readily available to you.)

Can you give me the names of people whose home studies you have done? (Some people may not want their names to be given out, and some home study professionals will not give out names to begin with.)

Marjorie had a funny vibe about the social worker, whom I'll call Ms. Match, who did her home study. They did not click and Marjorie left her interview feeling unhappy and uneasy. At a later time, when Marjorie bumped into Ms. Match at an adoption conference, Ms. Match didn't remember having met her.

Marjorie felt angry and resentful as a result, and put her adoption on hold while she assessed whether she wanted to carry on.

Home Study Fees Range Widely: Shop Around

You will find a wide range of quotes for non-agency home studies. Where I live, they ranged from $375 to $1,000, and sometimes higher. (The quotes for home studies by agencies tend to be much higher.) Some agencies include them in their fee packages without saying how much the home study represents; others tack on an extra fee for the service. Since I was using an out-of-state agency, I chose to work with a certified social worker who specializes in home studies, has links to that agency, and has been an adoption specialist for twenty years. I had met her at an adoption conference, where she had a display, but I was more impressed by the recommendations of people I knew who had used her service. In addition, I had an adoption counseling session with her prior to hiring her when I wanted to discuss my hesitancies and concerns about adoption. She spent a long time with me but charged a flat fee that she had quoted in advance.

Be choosy! Since you'll be baring your soul to the person who writes about you, you should select someone who makes you feel comfortable about your decisions regarding adoption and who you feel you can trust. You may also want to work with this person during the post-adoption phase.

What Type of Living Space Is Considered Acceptable?

The home study includes a review of your residence. You do not have to own a mansion. One friend of mine was accepted though she lives in a studio apartment. Another lives in a walk-up one-bedroom apartment, but has adapted it appropriately to accommodate her young daughter. If she can move to a larger place someday, she will, but if she can't, she already has ideas on how to allocate the space to make it work.

A good home study can make a valid assessment of the space depending on the person and the type of adoption, including the age and gender of the child. Smaller spaces such as the two I've just described are more likely to be acceptable if the child is the same gender as the adopting parent and is an infant or toddler when the adoption takes place.

What Factors Could Result in a Negative Home Study?

A history of child abuse and/or substance abuse could be liabilities to a positive recommendation to adopt. An unstable lifestyle, such as multiple marriages or frequent changes of job or residence, often can also work against an applicant. A couple with a wide difference in age range may also be rejected by the country of adoption. I read of just such a couple—the wife was in her mid-thirties and her husband in his sixties—who were having problems finding a country that would permit them to adopt. This does not have to be an obstacle in adopting if you truly offer a good and loving home for a child. International Concerns for Children (ICC) writes that if you are persistent, you will find an agency that can help you. Don't give up!

An unmarried couple is less likely to be considered acceptable than a single person adopting on his or her own or, for example, a household that contains other relatives who have indicated their intention to participate in raising the child. (In the case of lesbian and gay couples, the adoption is usually done by one member of the couple, and the other person will likely be described as a housemate who will participate in the child care.) Many gay couples are doing adoptions, but not openly, because of antigay bias by some foreign governments (see Chapter 9). Generally, couples should have been married two to three years in order to show that they have a stable relationship.

After the Home Study

A draft of the home study will be sent to you for review so that you can make corrections and add any necessary updates. If you request major additions and/or changes, your home-study writer may charge an extra fee for the work. This will not be the case if you are merely making corrections for factual misinterpretations or for typographical errors.

The corrected, completed home study will then be sent back to you. Keep a copy for your file and send the original to INS. This whole process should take just a few weeks from the date of the initial interview. (The woman who did my home study sent a copy of it to the agency I used. She took care of that mailing as a favor and because she had a history with the agency. But it was my responsibility to send the completed home study to INS.)

The INS file is complete when it contains the I-600A, proof of citizenship (at least of one person if you're part of a couple), the home study, a birth certificate, and fingerprint cards. INS will then have the FBI do a check of your background.

When you clear the FBI check and your file is finally complete, you will receive Form I-171H, which approves you as a candidate to complete an adoption. This form, which is good for eighteen months, will tell you the disposition of your I-600A. Most of the time it states that the form has been sent to the U.S. consulate or embassy of the country from which you will adopt your child. At the same time, your agency or facilitator will be working with its contacts in the host country to seek an assignment of the child who will become yours. (Note: If you were arrested or have a history of substance abuse, your home study preparer can assess your current suitability to adopt and write a letter of support to INS on your behalf.)

Immigration of Your Child

Upon approval to adopt and the assignment of a child, you still have to follow key procedures in order to bring the child home. Here is the checklist of follow-up tasks:

> *Immigrant visa for the child.* If the child is adopted abroad, it is IR-3; if the child is adopted in the United States, it is IR-4. The fee for this visa at this writing is $200, which must be paid for in local currency, U.S. cash dollars, a money order, cashier's check, or certified check. Neither credit cards nor personal checks are accepted. If you are adopting in the country, you will undergo an interview with the local consular officer. This process includes a "visual inspection" of the child. In China, I have heard that more than thirty adoptions are processed daily, and that they move along fairly smoothly. You might want to contact other parents to find out what their experiences have been.
>
> *Medical examination of the child by a designated physician approved by the U.S. consulate or embassy.* The main purpose of the exam is to find out if the child has a serious contagious disease or disability. If such a medical condition is detected, you might still get a visa for the child if you have it treated. But some fairly common problems of children adopted overseas, such as parasites, may not be so readily detected, and you should be on the alert for them. *Take your child to see a doctor right away when you get home.*

Recognizing Your Child's Adoption in the United States

If you did not travel to get your child, you will have to go to court in your state of residence to "readopt" your child; this will also enable you to get a state birth certificate, which will come in handy. This procedure may also be required if you traveled overseas and completed the requirements there, but only if your state has mandatory readoption. Your facilitator or agency can help you with this, or check with local social services agencies if you did the adoption on your own. (See also Chapter 7.)

Naturalizing Your Child

Your child will not become a U.S. citizen until you apply for citizenship on his or her behalf. There's no rush, but don't wait until your child turns eighteen, which is the deadline! To get this going, file INS Form N-643 (Application for Certificate of Citizenship on Behalf of an Adopted Child) in your state of residence.

4

Facing the Money Question

You've probably heard that international adoptions are very expensive. You may have heard quotes of $30,000 and even more. I have. A legal, legitimate adoption should never cost that much. Even if you can afford it, the experts will probably tell you to stay away.

Most legitimate international adoptions, with all expenses included, will cost in the range of $12,000 to $23,000, whether you use an agency or a facilitator. In either case, many of the same procedures and fees are required to compile your dossier and to complete the adoption. Many of you will also be asked to make a donation to the agency or orphanage where your child has been staying. Prices vary widely with different agencies and services. If you really shop around—and use the free adoption networks available to you for advice—you can save a lot of money. Agencies and facilitators will quote you a wide range of fees, but you must find out precisely what they are including in their quote—and what they're not telling you. (As I type this, I'm looking at a list of agencies that place children from Peru, and the fees quoted range from $5,000 to $18,000.)

In this chapter, I've put together a variety of strategies that can help you keep adoption costs down. Many of the prices I give you are very rough estimates, but they will provide you a ballpark figure of what you can expect to spend. Your own research should produce more precise numbers.

The cheapest way of all is to arrange the adoption yourself, without an intermediary. *But* you must have already identified a child whom you know is legally available for adoption, and you also must know the right channels and work directly with the institution and with the appropriate authorities within the country from which you are adopting. You may do this if you are able, through knowledgeable country contacts, to identify a child or children who are in an institution and have been established to be abandoned and are thus legally available for adoption. You must apply for approval to adopt that child. Your principal costs will be to open your INS file and processing fees in the United States, visa and processing fees in the country where you are adopting, and, most likely, a donation to the institution where the child or children have been staying.

My impression is that this type of adoption works best if you are from the country or have excellent contacts, such as relatives or government officials, whom you know very well and trust. As I mentioned earlier, my friend Teresa adopted directly from an orphanage in the Dominican Republic, drawing on assistance from relatives in the country who helped her make the contact and arranged for a local lawyer. She estimated her total costs at $6,000.

But it doesn't always work out smoothly or inexpensively. The bottom line is—as with everything in this process—BE IN-FORMED!

The variables depend on the choices you make in settling on an agency and on country-specific costs, and whether or not you are traveling. When you hear inflated costs, you will know that the money is being used neither to cover basic agency fees nor to help a foreign orphanage, but to enrich a lawyer and various of the lawyers' friends and contacts, including, sometimes, corrupt judges. Also, you may find that adoption fees are lower if you are willing to adopt a "special-needs" child or an older waiting child. The definition of special needs can vary widely; in some cases, a basic surgical procedure not available in the child's country of birth can remedy the situation. I have also heard of children being labeled as having special needs because of something no worse than a birthmark.

There are, unfortunately, people claiming to be adoption professionals who behave in unscrupulous ways and prey on the vulnerability of people desperate to adopt. A couple I know, having experienced years of infertility and the failure of one adoption effort, was informed that healthy Guatemalan infant twins were available for adoption if the parents could come up with $40,000. They had to make their decision that weekend. It was agonizing for them to have to say no. After all, here were children waiting for a home, and they had a home awaiting them. But, as the wife said, it didn't "smell" right. They were right to go with their intuition. You should never be forced to make such a choice under duress. Remember that there are many children waiting for homes, and you need to get the child who is right for you at the right time.

A good agency or facilitator will state its fees from the outset and itemize them so that you know how much is going to the agency/facilitator and how much is going to the orphanage where the child assigned to you is staying. Other fees will cover such tasks as medical examinations, document translation, document authorization, and foster care, if your child was placed with a local family prior to placement with you. You should find these out in advance. Some agencies may allow you to pay in installments. Ask!

"A la Carte" Agencies

I have also seen references to "à la carte" agencies that will only charge for those services it performs for you if you are willing to take on others. Such an agency can play the important role of establishing contact in the country where you are adopting and completing key paperwork that you would probably not be able to do easily. You, on the other hand, may be able to do some of the legwork or document collecting that the agency might otherwise charge you for. I have never seen a listing of such agencies per se, so you will have to make the inquiries yourself when you do the research. One man said that he ended up paying just $3,000 to his agency, not including the orphanage donation, by doing a lot of work himself. My agency fee was just under $5,000, not including the orphanage donation, and it did almost everything.

No matter how much you prepare, last-minute fees are sometimes thrown in that even your agency may not know about. Friends of mine who went to Russia to pick up their two-and-a-half-year-old son in 1992 were asked to pay $1,000 to the facilitator that their Washington, DC, agency had hired to act as their intermediary. They had not been told of this fee beforehand, and they had the feeling that this was a last-minute add-on at a vulnerable time. They did not protest. This situation is less likely to happen if you are in a large organized group that is adopting together. You will, however, probably be advised to bring gifts for your in-country facilitator and possibly the facilitator's family. For example, we were advised that our representative in China, who would be with us throughout our stay, also had an eleven-year-old son. I brought him a baseball and a baseball cap.

I've put together a checklist of some of the tasks you must or may have to do and their estimated cost. Some of the estimates range widely, and you must really shop around to find the service and cost that meet your particular needs. Some of these expenses will be ongoing investments in building adoption networks and your own knowledge about raising an adopted child.

Note: Many fees will vary depending on the state or municipality you live in and the type of service you choose. As part of your own networking process, you should also find out what other people in your community are spending, and be aware that fees may change following the publication of this book.

Must Do

For the dossier:

Home study	$375–$1,000+
INS application (I-600A) fee	$155 (as of 1/1/96)
Also for the dossier	$150–$500

    Fingerprints for INS file

    Birth certificate(s)

    Marriage certificate(s)/Divorce decree(s) (where it applies)

    Child abuse clearance

    Good conduct certificate (documentation from the police headquarters in your county attesting to a clean record)[1]

    Medical checkup and doctor's letter

---

[1] In New York City, I needed to show a sponsor's letter attesting to the fact that I was adopting a child to be able to get the good conduct certificate. This is not the case everywhere; a friend who adopted through a facilitator and also lived in New York City went to another county to get her certificate because there was no official letter. Another friend who also adopted in New York City was not asked for a sponsor's letter. She got the impression that the particular staff that day "didn't really care." But if you're going to make a special trip to get the certificate, check in advance to find out exactly what you need. I *didn't* know about the letter and had to make an extra trip as a result. It was a particularly nerve-wracking day for me, because I had to take a plane overseas later that evening and hadn't finished packing. It's usually that way, isn't it?

Notary fees
Accountant's letter (include charge for his/her time)
Miscellaneous[2]

To identify a child and do the adoption:
Agency application fee: $150–$500
Facilitator or agency fees: $3,000–$10,000+ (varies widely on either end)
Foreign lawyers' fees (if working with a facilitator or on your own): $5,000–$15,000+
Orphanage donation (if separate from the agency fee): $2,000–$4,000
Naturalization/embassy fees: $200 for child's visa
Child's medical checkup in the country of adoption: Varies with country

Optional

These are some additional possible expenses you may incur. I've listed their approximate range, and they can vary widely.

Adoption consultation: $100–$150
Annual membership in adoption organizations: $25–$50 each
Subscriptions to adoption-related publications: $15–$25
Subscription to online service: starts at $9.95 per month
Adoption-related books: $12+/paperback, $22+/hardcover
Adoption conferences and seminars: 0–$25

---

[2] Just when I thought all my paperwork was done, my agency called me to say that authorities in Beijing had added the requirement of a photograph of the building I live in. So there was the further cost of film and processing. Anxious as I was, I rushed off to my closest camera shop and bought a disposable camera and took photos of my building. This was in the midst of a blizzard. When I caught my breath, I realized I could wait a couple of days for the snow to melt and the sun to come out to take a better picture.

Travel expenses, depending on the country, length of stay, your means of travel, and the accommodations you choose: you should budget $1,500 per person at bare minimum; $2,500 to $3,000 and more if you choose higher-quality air travel and/or hotel accommodations. Break this cost down as follows:

- Airfare
- Ground transport
- Hotels
- Meals
- Tips
- Gifts and souvenirs
- Miscellaneous
- Emergency (medical/baby care items, etc.)

(Your agency may recommend a travel agency to arrange the trip and hotel reservations for you. You may not get the best rates this way. If this is a concern to you—and some hotels catering to American adoptive families are taking advantage by charging very high rates—you have the right to arrange your own travel. Although I had friends in Hong Kong who had made a standing offer for me to stay with them, I traveled with my group and accepted the travel agent's hotel recommendations because it seemed the path of least resistance. My credit card felt that for quite a while!)

Translation expenses can vary. Your agency may cover them, or you can find a translator at a university (less expensive), or through professional services (more expensive).

Lawyers' fees for contingency situations, if necessary. (I never needed one, and most people doing an international adoption do not.)

If You're Traveling

Always have extra cash on hand for unexpected fees and emergency expenses. Do *not* count on being able to use your credit card or checkbook for emergencies.

My Choices on Spending

I personally chose to have an adoption consultation for $150, because I felt lost in a sea of possibilities and needed guidance from an adoption professional. This was a positive experience for me, but you may not need it if you have already decided where and how you want to adopt. I was quoted this fee for the session. It lasted three hours, and I truly felt that it was worthwhile.

I then used this consultant to write my home study. Her fee was $500. She sent me a thorough list of her fees for all the services she provided, so there was no surprise. You should know all fees in advance!

I belong to several organizations, including a "generalist" organization, Adoptive Parents Committee (APC) ($25 annual membership); a support group, Families with Children from China (FCC) ($25 to join), and New York Singles Adoptive Children (NYSAC) ($25 membership fee). FCC offers cultural activities and an excellent newsletter full of information on concerns specific to Asian children. There is also a great calendar of cultural activities and ads for parents wanting to form playgroups or share child care. NYSAC offers a range of support information for single adoptive parents, including seminars and occasional social get-togethers.

I also joined a synagogue in my neighborhood. It has an array of family activities, including a single-parents' support group. I guess I'm a joining type, but you may not be.

Home-Study Costs

I have been surprised at the range of fees I've heard quoted for the home study. A friend found a social worker who charged only $375. Most quotes I've heard range from $400 to $1,000. One book I read cited costs of $1,000 to $2,000, and a couple told me that they had paid $3,000. Agencies that include home studies in their fee should tell you how much it represents of the total charges you will be asked to pay. The International Concerns for Children (ICC) *Report on Intercountry Adoption* lists the services and fees that agencies provide, although these are not broken down in much detail. In one case, it lists the adoption fees charged by a well-known agency at their lowest amount. It notes that the agency uses a sliding scale for its fees, but I believe the listing is misleading and unrealistic. I don't know anyone who has used that agency for a foreign adoption that has paid anything close to the low range cited in the report. (See also Chapter 3.)

FINANCIAL SUPPORT FOR ADOPTION

Tax Credit?

In 1996, the U.S. Congress passed legislation permitting adoptive parents to take a $5,000 tax credit to cover adoption costs. The credit will become effective as of January 1, 1997, and will apply to families with incomes of up to $75,000, and then be gradually phased out at an income ceiling of $115,000. Retroactive expenses are not covered.

Financial Assistance

A number of religious organizations have loan funds and many employers offer some form of support, but I've come across just one organization that actually gives grants that can assist with

foreign adoptions: National Adoption Foundation, 100 Mill
Plain Road, Danbury, CT 06811; phone: (203)791-3811; fax:
(203)791-3801.

Norman Goldberg, a retired business owner and the adoptive
father of a four-year-old (when we spoke), formed the National
Adoption Foundation (NAF) in 1994, he says, "because I had
done well in my life and I wanted to give something back."
With some of Goldberg's own money and contributions from
two colleagues on the NAF board, the foundation offers grants
between $1,000 and $2,500 to help those deemed in greatest
need. Grants are evaluated and awarded quarterly, and applicants who have been rejected may reapply. There is a one-time
application fee of $20. Some two hundred applicants had been
helped when we spoke. The main criterion, besides need, is a
completed home study—the type of adoption is not a consideration. The grant is *not* made to the applicant. When a grant
is awarded, it is placed in an escrow account to an agency or
an attorney and is released to reimburse expenses as they
take place. At this writing, this was the only outright grantor
organization I could identify that provides any form of assistance with international adoptions. NAF has aggressively adver-
tised and received many applications—and left many people
disappointed and bitter, according to some of the E-mail post-
ings I have read, especially because they had to pay a
nonrefundable application fee but got no help. However,
Goldberg claims that in its first two years the foundation dis-
bursed about $75,000.

NAF has also joined with NationsBank to create a credit line
to provide loans from $2,500 to $25,000 at 3.9 percent over
prime rate. NAF gives grants and has a revolvingloan fund that
is coordinated through NationsBank SA; call (800)448-7061 and
ask for information about the loan. You can also write to: National Adoption Foundation Loan Program, P.O. Box 17296,
Baltimore, MD 21298–9481.

You should also do the following:

• **Consult your employer.** A growing number of companies offer some form of help to families who adopt children. This can range from unpaid or paid time off (I got six weeks' paid maternity leave), in addition to what is already legally required under the Family Medical Leave Act, as well as resource and referral information on child care and financial support. Companies that do provide financial support generally offer between $2,000 and $4,000, with a few going as high as $6,000. You may have to allocate your vacation time for your trip and then take unpaid family leave. At the time that I was writing this book, Suzanne Kemp of the National Adoption Center in Philadelphia was conducting a survey of the adoption support provided by U.S. employers and had prepared a brochure entitled *Looking at the Business Case: Why Adoption Benefits?* Call 1-800-TO-ADOPT (862-3678) for information.

• **Places of worship.** Some places of worship have a loan fund or other type of family assistance program. Your church fund may be willing to help you with travel expenses or your fee. The Jewish Child Care Association in New York City has a fund, and you may discover others in your community.

• **Family assistance.** You're lucky if you have family members who support what you're doing and have the means to help. One woman told me that her sister gave her some of her frequent flyer miles when she and her husband went overseas to pick up the two children they adopted.

• **Credit card.** You can use your credit line to get an advance for your adoption. A growing number of agencies will accept your credit card to cover fees.

• **Bank loan.** If you have had a good relationship with your bank, you may be able to get a home equity loan that will help you cover your adoption expenses.

• **Refinancing your home or car.** If you have such an asset, this may be a way to get the cash you need to pay for your adoption, and then repay the loan over time.

• **Taking a loan against your 401(k).** If you work for a company that offers you a 401(k) pension plan—or in my case, with a nonprofit, which offers a 403(b)—you may have the right to take a loan against it. Inquire with your personnel department or the investment firm managing your account.

• **Adopting under the auspices of a charitable organization.** In the course of your research, you may find listings of charitable organizations that assist with adoptions and whose fees may be partly deductible because of their charitable status. At this time I have seen this only with reference to an organization involved with adoptions from Nepal.

• **Special-needs adoption.** You may be eligible for a reduced fee and/or some form of financial or therapeutic support if you adopt a special-needs child. Friends of mine who did such an adoption of a seven-month-old boy from Romania discovered a range of services available to them after the adoption, including physical therapy given at their home. These services, provided by New York State, were free, and their son, who is now three, is thriving.

• **Working out a payment plan with your agency; working with an à la carte agency.** As already mentioned, some agencies will permit you to spread out payment of your fees, and, while others, sometimes referred to as à la carte agencies (see also Chapter 2), will charge you only for the services they perform if you do the legwork.

5

The Long Wait

I can certainly understand if you feel daunted by everything you have to do to adopt a child. I did. Sometimes I paused on my paperwork and other tasks because I needed a breather. (An advantage of doing an adoption is that you *can* pause if you need to. You can even stop if you discover that it's not what you want.)

It's also possible that mistakes will be made in the course of the adoption—by you or someone else. I encountered three delays in my adoption, one that was my fault, another due to a delay by the Chinese bureaucracy, and a third for which the blame is uncertain.

In the first case, I had forgotten that I was supposed to send my corrected home study to INS. For some peculiar reason, I had thought that the social worker who wrote it had sent it in. This was never her responsibility, but I totally forgot. My approval never came through, but I got so wrapped up with other tasks, that I didn't even think about it until eight months later. By then—late 1995—the federal government had been shut down as the result of the failure of Congress to enact a new budget. I panicked. I discovered two things:

1. Despite the shutdown, the woman processing INS adoption files was still coming to work. God bless her! So things were moving along.
2. I also found out that although the original home study was more than six months old, I could resubmit it with an update, as long as my life situation had not changed dramatically, which it had not, and reactivate my file. I did this immediately—the update fee was just $80, and I also had to request a new child abuse clearance, for which I was not charged—and had my INS clearance within six weeks. Phew!

In the second case, I had gotten my travel date to China, only to learn that it was being postponed for "two or three weeks." It was then postponed again for a total delay of ten weeks. At first, I didn't mind the modest postponement: two more weekends when I could sleep late and extend my crash course in baby care. But I did mind *not* having a new departure date, because despite my earlier pauses, once I had gotten the approval—and especially once I had my daughter's photograph—I *wanted* her. There was nothing I could do except keep the faith that my agency was on top of the situation and working for me and the seven other families who were adopting in Suzhou with me. The agency has an excellent record, so I sat tight, and sometimes phoned other people in my group for an update and to commiserate (the agency had promptly faxed me a list of names and phone numbers at my request). Once a new departure date was finalized, the agony I'd experienced during the painful wait quickly receded.

The third case actually happened before the other blunders, but it was the worst. I had mailed in my first adoption application, which had a modest application fee, to get the ball rolling in

July 1995. For me, and perhaps for you, the process seemed like a ritual. I carefully folded my application into an envelope, checked and double-checked that I had addressed it properly, walked it to my local post office, weighed it to make sure there was enough postage, and mailed it from there.

It never arrived. It was never returned to me. I found this out three weeks later, just as I was getting ready to go overseas on business for a month. I only discovered this when I called my agency and found that they had no record of it. My agency was wonderful: they FedExed a new application packet to me so I had it the next morning. But I have to admit that the loss had an emotional impact on me. Do you think I'm nuts to suggest that it was equivalent to a miscarriage? It took me another three months to complete the new application. This time, I took it to the main post office in New York City and sent it by Express Mail. It arrived. I was on track again.

These things *do* happen.

So let's pause to examine what happens when the adoption process itself is stalled. It's also a good time to examine what can happen between the time you are notified that a child has been assigned to you (your referral) and, pending your approval of the referral, the go-ahead either for the trip you will take to get your child or the arrival of your child in the United States with an escort.

Often, the time between referral and the adoption can take several months, and up to a year or longer in exceptional cases. I have heard of adoptions taking place within weeks of a referral, but one woman who had that happen to her then ended up spending more than six months—not voluntarily—in Peru. Although she had her child days after arriving, she was not mentally or emotionally prepared for such a long stay. And her husband, who had flown down with her, had had to return home to resume his teaching job. In retrospect, she calls it a worthwhile experience, but she would rather not have had to go through it.

The long wait is a time that can be tremendously anxious, especially if something unexpected occurs to make it even longer. You may feel ready to take in your child and may have scheduled your work and other plans around your child's arrival. Family members are also waiting. You've adapted your home for your child. You've changed your lifestyle already. And you've been emotionally and mentally prepared for it. The letdown can be exhausting and very depressing.

But you're not alone—that's one important way to take solace. Because there can be delays, many adoption support groups have "waiting workshops" that counsel adoptive parents through this difficult time. These workshops also cater to parents seeking to do adoptions of newborns in the United States, for some of the emotional experiences are similar.

Certainly, you can use this time to prepare. You most definitely will not have much of it once you have your child. (I gave myself a full weekend just to clean closets. I hadn't done this in over a decade and stumbled on wonderful old photographs, magazines, and books I'd forgotten that I had—and also threw out tons of stuff.) This is a good time, also, to acquire furniture and clothing that your child will need. Your family and friends probably know that you're adopting and will also want to help out.

If you've never raised a child before, this is also a good time to take classes in basic child care. It hadn't occurred to me to do this while I was waiting until someone else suggested it. What a great idea!

In foreign adoptions, delays in getting either a referral or the final approval to travel may happen for different reasons.

• Your dossier may not be complete.
• Your home study may not be considered appropriate. I've heard of home studies being rejected because they were not written to suit the country's key concerns.
• The country you are working with may amend its dossier requirements.

- Your agency or facilitator may not have the firm contacts in the country you are hoping to adopt from and is taking longer than promised to get an assignment.
- Your agency may have given you an unrealistic timetable (some agencies do this as a way to attract clients; this is why you *need to do independent checking*).
- Laws in that country are about to change or have just changed.
- As a result of those changes, some countries may put a moratorium on adoptions.
- Questions about whether the child has been legitimately "abandoned" may arise and need to be investigated (I have heard this particularly with reference to some Indian adoptions).

In short, you may find that completing your adoption takes far longer than you had planned. This can be frustrating, potentially traumatic and emotionally draining, especially as you try to plan your life and try to explain to the people who care about you and know about the adoption why you still don't have a child. You may even feel a bit out of control for a while. This is a term I have heard many parents use. I went through it myself. The most obvious symptom was insomnia.

Although you cannot predict everything that will occur, you can avoid some of these delays by making sure that the agency or facilitator you are working with has done many *recent* placements from the country, and also has a contingency plan for you in case something drastic happens and the adoption falls through. Get the agency's guarantee on this in writing as well as referrals!

ALICE'S STORY:
HANDLING A LONG DELAY ALONE

Alice, the lawyer mentioned earlier whose adoption is described in greater detail in Chapter 9, had set out to adopt an older child, first domestically, and then internationally when she found after much back-and-forth with state authorities that single mothers were considered candidates to adopt only as a last resort. In addition to doing extensive research (she found ICC's *Report on Intercountry Adoption* of particular value) and writing to about two dozen agencies, she also took part in adoption news groups on the Internet, as well as the commercial services such as America Online and Prodigy. As a result of these contacts, she found out about, and eventually signed with, the agency through which she was able to arrange for her adoption of Nadia.

Alice particularly liked the fact that the agency sends videos and photographs of waiting children even *before* a client signs up. After seeing a photograph of a little Russian girl, Alice asked to see her video. She fell in love. The service matched her to the agency responsible for this child. It was happy to work with a client willing to take in an older child. By this time—in mid-1994—Alice had already opened her INS file and completed a home study, hoping that once she had identified a child to adopt and the adoption was approved, she could get the wheels moving quickly. She also liked the fact that the agency fees were relatively low for a Russian adoption, about $11,700, not including travel, her home study, and various small tasks. Many agencies were asking much higher fees. Alice refinanced her car to raise most of the payment.

However, beginning in July 1995 she faced several delays in traveling to Russia to pick up her daughter when the Russian government announced that it would be changing its rules regarding the placement of children. The new rules went into effect the following September. They entailed the creation of a "central list" of adoptable children for placement with Russian families. Children under three would be on the list for three months before they could be released for foreign adoption. Children over three would be on the list for six months.

"I didn't think it would apply to Nadia, because she had already been assigned to me," Alice says. "But I was wrong." The agency told her from the beginning that she would be able to go in October, then November, then December. Absolutely on December 22nd, it said. She imagined traveling in mid-January.

When the delays first started, Alice asked the agency if she could, at least, begin communicating with Nadia. She sent cards to her through the agency representative in Moscow. And to friends who were traveling to complete their own adoptions, she asked them to give Nadia gift packages and a tape recorder with a cassette of her voice.

By December 22, Alice was told Nadia would be on the March list. "This was the most depressing moment for me because I had already bonded with her," she told me. "I fantasized that I could go over and just fix it."

She got through it in several ways. For one thing, the Russian "mailing list" on the Internet provided enormous support. She could correspond on the open forum and share her worries and anguish, and also carry on private correspondences with individual participants. There were families in California and Virginia who became close friends this way. And she found a family in her own city in Florida that was about to adopt a nine-year-old Russian boy. She painted and decorated the room in her house that she had set aside for Nadia. She also took private lessons in Russian from a Russian student at the local university and began making friends with Russian people in her community.

To make the situation worse, Alice had to make two trips to Russia, once before the adoption was finalized and the second in order to finalize it. This was the result of changes enacted by the city of Moscow government and in some other parts of Russia, though not all, requiring that the adoptive parent or parents see the child before the adoption application can be filed and that the adopting parent(s) be present to file the application. The application is then processed in a period of three to five weeks. The adoptive parents may wait in Moscow or, as Alice chose to do, go home and then return when the application is nearly complete. The long wait, which is not required elsewhere in Russia (although you should find out explicitly what *is* required in the region or city from which you are adopting), added another $2,500 to her cost.

BETHANY AND KARL:
A VERY ANXIOUS YEAR

In January 1995, after a nine-month wait for a referral, Bethany and Karl were assigned a six-month-old girl in an orphanage in Hyderabad, India. They planned to name her Adina. With the dossier complete and the assignment approved, they now waited for the thumbs-up to take the trip. Most adoptions from India are done with escorts, Bethany told me, but she had her sights on going to India herself.

One hitch: the U.S. consular official in Hyderabad suspected that the "abandoned" status of some of the children being placed in homes was questionable because of a history of fraud in the area, and her office undertook detailed investigations of each child that had been assigned. Many adoptions were held up as a result, some for two years and longer. "We were all in contact," Bethany told me while she was still waiting. "We have a support group of families and I've started a newsletter to help us stay in contact." They also found out about conditions in the orphanage from parents who were able to go over. They could arrange to have gifts brought to their children and have pictures taken "and to see that they get hugged."

Bethany expected first to go over in April of that year, and then in June. By then, the cases of twenty-six children were being investigated. "The difficult part is going up and down. The dam is breaking, I think. Soon she'll come." But still, a delay. Some parents had been waiting for two years, Bethany told me. Some families couldn't take the wait and backed out. Even the agency that was supposed to be helping was at a loss. The situation was out of their hands.

Finally, the word came through in January 1996 that Bethany could go and get Adina. During their waiting time, Adina had grown from being a tiny infant to an eighteen month-old toddler. (Bethany and Karl also have two birth sons, and Karl stayed home with them.) Bethany was in India for three weeks but had custody of Adina the day after she arrived.

6

The Last Step—But Just the Beginning

You've had your referral and now the time has arrived for you to bring your child into your home. This will happen either by traveling abroad to pick up your child or through an escort arrangement with your agency or facilitator to bring the child to the United States. This chapter examines:

1. What you need to do to complete the adoption
2. Special suggestions if you travel
3. Health tips for your trip

1. COMPLETING THE ADOPTION

Whether or not you travel to get your child, you or the facilitator or agency working on your behalf will have to collect more documents to complete the adoption, as well as obtain a visa (Form OF 230) so your child can enter the United States.

These include:

- a passport for your child from the country of his or her birth
- photographs of your child
- a completed and signed medical examination report from a physician endorsed by the consulate.
- the I-604 Report on Overseas Orphan Investigation Form, which will be completed by the local consular officer when your child is undergoing the medical examination. This is an important step leading to the final approval (I-600 Form).
- a visa application form OF 230
- the completed I-600 form (Petition to Classify an Orphan as an Immediate Relative) if you filed an I-600A and it is with the consulate. (You received a blank I-600 with your I-600A and should have kept it on file. Otherwise, speak to your agency or contact INS for a new copy.)

In conventional adoptions where the paperwork and the local consulate is well organized (i.e., following the guidelines of the State Department's Office of Children's Issues), this process may take just twenty-four hours. If you're part of a group of parents adopting in a place like China where several dozen adoptions are processed each workday, this should not be a hassle. However, more recently, because of increased volume, I have heard that the processing may require an extra day or two.

There are, of course, occasions when the paperwork is incomplete or there may be inconsistencies and the visa is not granted. You may want to have a plan B in such a situation, for example, an adoption lawyer on call just in case, although that does not guarantee a solution. I have heard especially of situations in India in which the final authorization was delayed for a year or longer because of uncertainty of the child's actual status as an "orphan," even though the adoptive parents working legitimately through agencies had been assigned to children and accepted the assignment. This may be due to concerns about potential fraud.

There are cases in which children are legally available for adoption even though one or both parents are alive. Such situations may arise because the parent(s) are unable to care for them. (Knowledge of the whereabouts of the parent(s) can help you if you ever need to know your child's medical history.) As long as both parents attest to this (or the child's mother says so if the father is unknown), it is considered a legitimate abandonment and the child may be placed for adoption. (I have heard of this in Romanian and African adoptions.) To prevent getting into a painful situation and a long delay, you should thoroughly investigate recent patterns of adoption in the country you wish to go to and the track record of your agency in completing adoptions in that country. And, of course, contact other adoptive parents who have done the type of adoption you wish to do. (Thank goodness for the on-line services. You'll get more honest responses by contacting people directly than you would if you asked your agency for referrals.)

If your child is escorted to you, then the facilitator or agency working on your behalf will obtain the documents that your child will need.

2. GUIDELINES IF YOU TRAVEL

Many countries require you to travel, sometimes more than once. The need to travel—and, in some cases, make a second trip—not only varies with the country but with the agency. When I was researching this book, I'd heard conflicting accounts relating to Russian adoptions, some people reported having to do one trip, others two. If an agency has excellent contacts in the country, it can sometimes arrange for them to do some of the advance paperwork you would have done on a first trip. You will, of course, pay for that service, but you won't have to disrupt your routine at home or work twice to do the adoption and also pay the extra plane fare and expenses.

But you usually don't save much money if you don't travel, because you will pay an escort fee when your child is brought to you. Ultimately, whether or not you travel depends on the country requirement and the choices you make. It may also depend on whether your employer gives you enough time off. In some instances, given your particular situation, you may find yourself overseas longer than planned.

I love to travel, so for me going to China to get my child was one of the most wonderful and exciting aspects of the process. I also felt that it would help me understand more about my child's background and also enable me to chronicle the journey that she took to become part of my family. Almost anyone who has taken the trip will recommend it—even though you can run into all kinds of problems.

Bethany, who has had two biological children, describes her trip to India to pick up her daughter as the equivalent of going into labor. There was lots of anguish in advance of her departure and the process itself was grueling and very time-consuming. But there was also considerable ecstasy in at last picking up her child in India and a special thrill in having taken the trip. The adoption had been delayed for one year—her daughter was six months at the time of the assignment and eighteen months old when she was finally adopted—so Bethany was particularly gratified when the process was over. "I love India and really want to go back," she now says. In her case, the wait had been painfully long, but she was not alone. When I was doing the research for this book, some Indian adoptions were taking many months and even well over a year to be completed because of extensive red tape that was *not* the fault of the agencies involved. Some of the red tape was due to U.S. bureaucracy, which, when I spoke to Bethany, was being looked into.

Pete and Patti went to Vietnam to get their twin sons. They

shortly picked up minor ailments from their sons. "You know how people say you get to look like your children?" Patti joked. "We each got conjunctivitis and our eyes looked a bit Asian!" Then, to top off the challenge of schlepping two babies home, their direct flight to their home city entailed *four* plane changes. No easy task for the new, and very tired, parents of twin sons.

Preparing to Travel

• **Travel with someone.** Whether you're going in a group or on your own, that person—a spouse, other relative, or friend—can provide emotional support as well as a spare pair of hands to take some of the load and give you a break. You will need it. It's also a way for you to share the experience with someone you're close to. Make sure this is someone you can feel comfortable with in close quarters for up to two weeks. This will be an intense and strange experience—I often hear people use the word "surreal." Your traveling companion should be someone who won't resent being needed so much or not having the time to go touring because you require help.

I had planned to travel with my mother, who broached it to me before I even approached her. I had not thought of her as an adventurous traveler, but she didn't make her offer because she wanted to see the Great Wall. She wanted to help me. An illness in my family prevented her from going, but one of my closest friends then offered to go along. We know each other well and have traveled together before. That made an enormous difference.

• **Be prepared for local weather conditions.** In a country as large as China, weather can vary according to the region you'll be going to. So it helps, for instance, to know whether to bring lightweight summer clothing or layered clothes for a cooler climate. The State Department has an advisory service that can help you with this. You can also contact the country's consulate.

• **Take pictures of your journey.** I don't have to tell you that, of course. But a very good pointer from people I spoke to, and took advice from, was also to bring a Polaroid camera. Instant pictures can serve as a wonderful gift, especially to orphanage caretakers who have been close to your child. Often we promise to send pictures, but then get too busy with our new responsibilities to get around to doing it. *Bring plenty of film.* You may *think* it's available in the country, and maybe it is. But it might not be the right kind or it could be horribly expensive— or it could be difficult to process in the United States. Some people also bring video cameras.

• **Bring a phrase book or take a basic course in the language of the country you'll be visiting.** Even if you stumble over the few words you know, people tend to be more appreciative of you and helpful if they see that you're at least trying to communicate on their terms and not forcing them to try to understand you. It's the Ugly American syndrome that I regret to have seen a few too many times. An American tourist seems to feel that if he raises his voice, the non-English-speaking person he's trying to talk to will miraculously understand him. (See also Chapter 9, "When Alice Met Nadia.")

• **What to bring.** The following composite list is drawn from a number of packing lists I've collected and from suggestions that people have made. You should try to minimize your packing, especially since you may want to buy clothing and souvenirs in the country you're going to. Obviously, if you are adopting an infant, some of the space in your luggage will be liberated as you use up diapers, formula, and other products you brought along.

For yourself:

Documents (do *not* pack your documents; assemble them in a knapsack or portfolio that you will keep on hand at all times)

Passport, tickets, travel insurance
Cash, credit cards, travelers' checks
Travel details (itinerary, hotels, flights, and emergency contact phone numbers)
Extra passport photos and copies of first page of passport
Phone and fax numbers of secretary of state and state representative
Copies of most recent 1040's
Extra copies of dossier documents, including I-171H, I-600A, I-600 (to be completed in the U.S. consulate abroad)
Stationery with personal letterhead
Photo ID, business cards
Contact numbers of family members
Calling card (AT&T USA Direct codes, if possible)

Clothing (keep it to a minimum; no-iron, drip-dry is recommended)
Pajamas or nightgown, and a few changes of underwear
One good outfit for consular and orphanage/caregiver's visit
Comfortable clothing for free days; one pair of "good" shoes, plus comfortable walking shoes
Sun hat
Winter clothing as necessary
For hot climates, sandals or flip-flops may be appropriate for walking around
Bathing suit
Note: In many countries, short shorts and skimpy T-shirts are inappropriate.

Personal care items
Standard first-aid items, plus prescription medications, Tylenol, etc.
Sunscreen, throat lozenges, insect repellent

Toiletries (tooth-care and hair-care items; tampons; shaving needs; contact lens paraphernalia; bath soap—don't count on hotels to provide it, although they may)
Extra tissue (doubles as toilet paper)
Washcloths

Miscellaneous
Alarm clock
Flashlight, portable shortwave radio
Batteries
Swiss army knife
Cameras and film
Polaroid camera, if possible
Photographs of you and your family to show your hosts
Granola bars, fruit bars, peanut crackers, and other portable dried food
Water purification tablets
Chewable Pepto-Bismol
Laundry soap, clothesline, clothespins
Miscellaneous fasteners: safety pins, rubber bands, tape
Headrest for travel
Fanny pack
Luggage trolley or a suitcase with built-in wheels
Extra-lightweight duffel

For your child:

Age-appropriate clothing (sleepers as well as day outfits)
Diapers (check on the size you will need)
Balmex (in case of diaper rash; clean and dry air is also good, although it may not be practical for your baby to be bare bottomed; check that others brands have zinc oxide)

Cotton balls, Q-tips

Diaper bag

Infant or children's medication: Baby Tylenol, medications for ear infections, lice, scabies, conjunctivitis, etc. (see a pediatrician before you go)

Formula (recommended: lactose-free powdered formula; a 14-ounce can lasts for three days)

Bottles, nipples (recommended: four 8-ounce plastic bottles)

Container or bottle to mix formula

Instant baby cereal and feeding spoon

Sugar packets

Sippy cup with spout for older babies

Bibs

Socks, booties

Sun hat

Baby carrier

Baby blanket

Crib sheets, waterproof pad

"Sassy" tub or inflatable pool (doubles as a baby bed)

Age-appropriate toys (I suggest a mirror)

Portable stroller (the on-line Chinese adoption newsgroup had a long debate on whether or not to bring strollers; parents who had completed their adoptions there generally opposed their use, but this would also depend on the age of your child, who might be too big for a Snugli-style baby carrier. I brought a very inexpensive stroller because I planned extra time in Hong Kong before going home)

Handi Wipes (I was advised to buy the refill packages rather than those in solid containers to save space, and to wrap open packages in Ziploc bags to preserve the moisture)

A small knapsack for an older child to tote things, possibly sunglasses

What to Bring for the Orphanage

Before your child was assigned to you, he or she was in an institution. You may be in a fortunate situation where your child has been fostered out for a period once he or she was assigned to you. But as part of your adoption fee, you will probably be required to make a donation to the orphanage that cared for your child. If you're able to visit it, you may also want to bring along some gifts.

For the adults, who are mostly women, these can include sewing kits, simple jewelry, soaps, cosmetics, cologne, hair-care items, postcards of where you come from, picture books, calendars, pins, key chains, pens, and other mementos, and decorative postage stamps.

Gifts for the children that are recommended by Judi Kloper, who has adopted older children, include small, flat toys (puzzles, coloring books, colored pencils, crayons, and paint sets), hard candies, Superballs for boys, hair barrettes for girls, paint brushes, kazoos, playing cards, as well as extra baby-care items that you will not need.

Questions to Ask Your Child's Care Provider

A friend of mine who adopted from China wrote a letter about her experience that she sends to other parents who will be traveling to get their child. She includes a list of questions to ask to the child's care provider. I am reproducing those questions here (with some cuts). Bear in mind that in China most placements are girls, but the questions apply equally to boys.

- What do you feed her? How much and when? Food first or milk? What temperature is the food or milk? How is it prepared?
- How long and when does she sleep? On her back, side, or (for noninfants) tummy?

- When and how does she go to the bathroom?
- Has she had any prior illnesses, accidents, or injuries?
- How do you bathe her? How do you hold her? How does she eat? (My friend's daughter, nine months old when adopted, could already hold chopsticks!)
- What makes her happy? What toys, games, or songs does she like?
- What makes her angry or upset? How do you calm or soothe her?
- What is her story? Where and how was she found or brought to the orphanage? (If you can, take a picture of the place. This will be wonderful for your child later on. My friend got photocopies of the police report describing when her daughter was found.)
- Who named her? How was the name chosen?
- What is the story of her foster family? If possible, get their names and addresses, and take their pictures.
- Are there any mementos of her life that you can keep? (My friend got a small towel that her daughter slept on and a small red top.)
- What religion was she involved with, if at all?

Also be prepared to let the care givers ask you questions about yourself: where you live, how old you are, why you are adopting from this country, and so on.

The Moment You Meet Your Child

Do bells go off? Does bonding happen right away? Usually, no. I've heard various stories of parents meeting their children and, in the case of a two-year-old Russian boy, the child running away and crying. In other cases, your infant child may simply scream. "One of the most common misperceptions is that this is going to be an awesome moment, but it is rarely like what you imagine, so don't worry," a friend says. Actually, you may be too stunned to think about bells and gurgles, that's what I hear often. Denise, mother of two sisters adopted at ages five and six from Hungary, admits that she bonded more quickly with the older daughter, while it took almost a year to feel fully bonded with the younger one. Very favored by her foster mother, who created a horrible situation for everyone by telling the two girls that she was their biological mother, the younger girl took longer to let herself get close to Denise. But now, three years later, along with their father, John, they are a close-knit family.

What to Take Home

Take advantage of your stay to buy:

- Toys, children's books, and souvenirs that are part of your child's culture and will remind your child of where he or she came from and when you picked him or her up. (If you have other children, buy toys and souvenirs especially for them, too.)
- Clothing from that country for your child(ren), yourself, and spouse.
- Music audiocassettes.
- A local newspaper or a magazine—even if you can't read it—as a souvenir of the day you met your child.
- A special souvenir for your child, such as a bracelet with your child's name in his or her language (a Chinese chop, or stamp, with your child's name in Chinese characters is one example). This will certainly be invaluable years later.
- If you can, take time to get to know the city or town where you picked up your child so that you can describe it and show him or her pictures.
- Bring a blank journal to record your experiences. This is also a wonderful gift to give someone who is about

to travel and may be too frantic to think about it in advance.

Possibly Your Last Vacation for a While

A number of people advised me to take time on my own in China to see sights and relax, if at all possible, before picking up my daughter.

Your trip will be important to you and your child when he or she grows older and wants more information on where he or she came from. Your chronicle of the trip will add to your child's pride and sense of history. And once you're involved in child raising, it may be a while before you get to take such a trip again. So if you have time, use your trip to do some sight-seeing, too.

My headstrong and bargain-conscious friend Nicole chose an unconventional way to fly between the United States and Hong Kong en route to China: she took a low-cost courier flight, which meant that she was not supposed to have any checked luggage in either direction. "My baby was carry-on," she quips, noting that her five-month-old daughter spent much of the trip in a Snugli, and Nicole made limited purchases during her stay. Still, even the courier company turned out to be flexible when Nicole turned up with the baby for her return trip home and let her check in a few items, such as a stroller. The company also accommodated her with a bulkhead seat.

Many travelers to China go directly to Beijing. Hong Kong offers you a good transition and a pleasant tourist stay before and after your time in China. You can also find inexpensive clothing and other goods to take home.

There are a number of agencies that assist adopting parents with their trips; they can get good fares and also help you get good seats. *Adoptive Families* magazine carries advertisements for these and your local adoption support group and agency can probably recommend some. A word of advice: Ask to speak to other people who have used a particular service before you sign on.

Remember, the Trip Is Your Child's Experience, Too

Until I read Susan Laning's paper "The Socialization of the Adopted Child" (see Chapter 1), I hadn't given much thought to the impact of the long airplane trip on the adopted child. This in itself is a major change in your child's life, and it's important to provide as much comfort as possible. Also, don't be surprised if your child has difficulty adopting to the new time zone and sleeping at night. You'll be jet-lagged, too.

When Denise and John went to Hungary to adopt their two daughters, then five and six, they worried about how the girls would react to the long trip from their small village in eastern Hungary to the United States. So first they went to Lake Balaton, a resort area in western Hungary, to spend some time together and get to know each other. "It was their first time away from their village and they thought *this* was America," says Denise. In fact, the plane ride was a great adventure for them. The staff gave them all sorts of toys and they had a wonderful time.

3. HEALTH TIPS FOR YOUR TRIP

Dr. Jerri Ann Jenista[1] is one of the most prolific authors on health issues connected to adoption. An excellent article she wrote was included with the packet of material I received from ICC and targets parents planning to escort their children home. I consider it essential reading to help you prepare—and you don't

---

[1] I wish to credit the International Concerns for Children in Boulder, Colorado, which sent me Dr. Jenista's untitled article, for the information included in this section.

have to be a medical genius to understand it. Jenista, mother of four adopted children, explains some of the potential health problems you might encounter in the countries where adoptions take place. She also provides a health-travel checklist to advise you on medications to take with you, just in case, and what some of the rashes you may see might actually be. She offers simple advice like taking anti-scabies lotion and anti-lice shampoo. Such advice as buying specific brands that happen to be prescription medications rather than over-the-counter products can only come from an experienced professional, and it's worth being well prepared.

Here is Jenista's checklist for your pretravel plans and education:

- Check your immunizations. The routine childhood ones are most important.
- Don't forget your medicines. If you need malaria prophylaxis (unnecessary in most countries where adoptions take place), you have to start before you travel.
- Use your common sense.
- If you wouldn't touch it, eat it, or drink it at home, don't do it there.
- If you wouldn't do it at home, don't do it there.
- Eat only hot food or food you prepare or peel yourself.
- Pick a bottled or hot drink and stick to it consistently.
- Wash your hands.
- Avoid mosquitoes.
- When you become ill at home, remind your doctor where you have been.

Avoiding the Ugly American Syndrome

A number of people I've spoken to have commented about feeling embarrassed when traveling with other Americans who were either loud and obnoxious, very demanding of their hosts, complained if there seemed to be a "flaw" with their children, criticized poor service or the less-than-luxury accommodations that they had, or portrayed themselves as heroes for adopting poor children from overseas. An adoption professional I know complains about a trend among some couples who come to her for advice and appear to be undertaking adoption in the same way that they would shop for a car.

It's true that as adoptive parents, we are indeed consumers looking for the right adoption service to help us meet our goal. But we are also trying to form families and seeking a child we can love and who will enrich our lives as well. In choosing an international adoption, we are going into a different culture. It is important to respect the culture and the traditions of the people in whose country we are guests.

If you can accept that, you will enjoy your experience and be very much expanded by it. Your child, however, is a vulnerable human being and has not been manufactured or customized to order. There is no way to request a perfectly healthy, brilliant child from the outset. If you were to give birth, there would be no guarantee, either.

7

You're Home!

Yes, you've made it through the system, and you and your child are now a family. Now the *real* work begins. And the fun, too! There are a few basic tasks you will have to think about. The most immediate one is your child's health. When things have settled down a bit, you will also want to think about post-placement reports, getting your child a social security number, re-adoption under U.S. jurisdiction, and obtaining citizenship for your child.

1. MEDICAL CONCERNS

The first task you must do is take your child to a pediatrician. If you haven't already found one, use your networks and do it now.

Almost all of us who adopt internationally are adopting children from impoverished backgrounds with a history of time spent in an institution. This situation immediately puts our children at a disadvantage compared with children of the same age who have always been with one family. Furthermore, many of our children are used to different types of nourishment (including undernourishment) and may have been exposed to rashes and parasites that require prompt treatment upon arrival home. Does it mean you should worry about his or her physical and emotional health and development?

Concerned, yes. All parents have to be concerned about their child's health and development. Always. But worried? That depends. There can be serious health and developmental issues when you adopt a child from overseas, in part because of the conditions under which your child was born and then the conditions under which he or she was raised until you came along. If you are working with a reputable agency that has excellent country contacts and has done many prior placements from the orphanage where your child has been staying, you will probably be able to get some information about your child's upbringing. Some Chinese orphanages foster out the children who have been assigned to families before they are placed; the fostering helps the children develop better opportunities to attach.

Depending on where you adopt, you may find that your child's problems are as basic as lack of dental care (parents I've spoken to who adopted older children from Bulgaria and Hungary have mentioned this to me), or parasites and rashes that can be easily treated. Other conditions may be more serious, such as the hepatitis B virus and, possibly, tuberculosis. If you have chosen to adopt a special-needs child, you should already be made aware of the child's condition and how it can be treated.

In some countries, there is contact with the birth families and you may be able to find out family medical histories, but this is not always the case, particularly if your child was abandoned. (A friend of mine named Nanette, who adopted her daughter, Polly, from Guatemala, told me that she doesn't worry about this problem even though she has no information on Polly's parents, because modern DNA testing can now provide key information that was once unavailable.)

`You will find that the countries that have children available for adoption are also those in which health problems and malnutrition are more common than in the United States and where infrastructures are lacking. This is no surprise. Poverty breeds these types of problems. And the children who have been abandoned are often the most disadvantaged in countries that are already poor. However, the care of *some* institutionalized children in *some* countries is of good quality. I have heard positive reports of some orphanages in Bulgaria and Russia, and, as more adoption support money comes in, conditions may well improve, and to an extent already have, in countries such as China and Vietnam. In some cases, this depends on the agency you are working with. The Vietnamese government matches agencies with certain orphanages, and, to some extent, your agency fees help support the particular orphanage. But you should familiarize yourself with the potential problems that your child may have, and talk to other parents who have adopted from the country your child comes from.

Fortunately, as more people adopt internationally, research and knowledge on adoption health issues is increasing. Two excellent resources are Dr. Dana Johnson, who heads the International Adoption Clinic at the University of Minnesota, and mentioned earlier, Dr. Jerri Ann Jenista in the department of pediatrics at the University of Michigan. Both have published widely, and you will find articles by them in *Adoptive Parents* magazine and ICC publications. Both are also adoptive parents. (See Appendix for contact information.)

Furthermore, as adoptions in countries such as China become more common, more information is becoming available to parents. Soon after my referral came through in July 1996 for a seven-month-old girl, I received an issue of the *Families with Children from China* newsletter from my local chapter (Greater

New York, Connecticut, New Jersey) with a cover article entitled "Facing Delays Head-on: The Promise of Early Intervention," by Priscilla Scherer. This topic has been a great concern to parents adopting from China, but until the article appeared, I had not seen so much good information on it in one place. What excellent timing for me! Scherer related her own observations about the difficulties her eight-and-a-half-month-old daughter encountered and her own denial that her daughter might benefit from extra help. She also provided a listing of Early Childhood Direction Centers throughout New York City that offer free services. You can also call the state education department or school district in your community as well as hospitals that may have evaluation and therapy programs to find out about such centers and treatment near your home.

The FCC newsletter offers this list of questions for you to consider as you evaluate your child's need for a developmental head start. Does he or she

- React with extreme sensitivity and fear to loud noises, bright light, or certain smells?
- Hate being touched or held; dislike crowds?
- Struggle a lot against changing clothes; show extreme irritation to the feeling of certain clothes or clothing labels?
- Actively struggle against having hair combed or washed?
- Hate having hands or feet dirty?
- Have unpredictable and lengthy emotional outbursts that are very difficult to bring to an end?

You might also want to see the extent to which your child

- follows hand moves
- develops speech patterns
- holds him/herself up

- interacts with you, other people, and things in his or her environment.

Your child might have what is referred to as sensory integration disorder, which may lead to learning problems when he or she begins school if these are not addressed during the ideal treatment period, namely, when he or she is very young

Early intervention assessment and therapy programs are federally funded and free of charge. If you have the opportunity to avail yourself of a consultation and, if necessary, therapy for your child, you may be able to collapse the time necessary to bring your child to his or her appropriate milestones. I know that some parents disagree on whether or not to do this. My friend Bettina, who adopted a nine-month-old from China, said that all you really need to do is focus on your child and give her a lot of love. Bettina's daughter, now almost three, is "on target," although it took a while. (She was the size of a three-month-old when Bettina adopted her.) But Priscilla Scherer indicates that she wishes she had intervened with her daughter much sooner. She could see the difference between her daughter and those children whose parents had taken advantage of therapy support.

In many cases, you will not need to seek special treatment, and a number of parents I interviewed said that they were satisfied with the knowledge and services provided by their local pediatrician, who was not experienced with children adopted internationally.

When You Adopt an Older Child

Sometimes when you adopt a somewhat older child, you may face developmental and emotional issues that may include inappropriate behavior such as acting out, tantrums, ongoing "testing" of you and other people he or she meets, an immature personality, poor reasoning skills and performance in school, and an inability to bond with you or other people. Certainly, your child must make an enormous adjustment, and although many parents report a honeymoon period soon after the adoption, the actual acclimatization to a new life may take longer. This is by no means the case with all older children: many adjust very well to their new homes, learn English with amazing speed, and become well integrated into their new families and community (see Chapter 9). But for some children, the toll of living in an institution for much of their young lives has left them craving attention, but showing inappropriate behavior, especially an inability to bond with family members or other people who are constants in the child's life, such as a teacher or a neighbor or a classmate. This attachment disorder may be the result of a combination of factors:

- your child's family life prior to institutionalization
- the institutionalization itself, including inferior health care and nutrition, inadequate individual attention, and unstimulating surroundings that contribute to the lack of appropriate physical and mental development, consistent changes in the care givers who attended to your child, and the need to learn survival strategies in a non-nurturing institutional environment

If you feel your child may benefit from an evaluation leading to appropriate treatment (such as psychological counseling or physical or occupational therapy related to this disorder), there are a number of organizations that will help you. They include the Attachment Disorder Parents Network in Boulder, Colorado, at (303)443-1446; Attach in Dallas, Texas, at (214)247-2320; the Attachment Center in Evergreen, Colorado, at (303)674-1910; and the Parent Network for Post-Institutionalized Children in Meadowlands, Pennsylvania, at (412)222-6009 or (412)222-1766. You can obtain *Sensory Defensiveness in Children Aged 2–12: An Intervention Guide for Parents and Other*

Caretakers by Patricia and Julia Wilbarger by contacting Avanti Educational Programs, Denver, Colorado, at (303)782-5117. America Online has a discussion group on attachment disorder issues, though many of the cases refer to U.S.-born children who have been in and out of foster care. But many issues are similar. The International Adoption Clinic in Minneapolis, Minnesota, is doing research in this area (see Appendix).

When I was writing this book, there were a number of reported cases of older children with particularly flagrant disabilities who had been placed with families in the United States who were not prepared for this. It turned out that the medical reports the parents received concealed the nature of their children's disorders, although it was discovered that the medical personnel responsible for the children was fully aware of them. At times, such adoptions may be disrupted, that is, the children are "returned" to the agency that placed them, and lawsuits have been filed charging the agencies with fraud.[1] As I write this, I know of no outcome to these suits nor of any policies to protect parents against such fraud. The agencies themselves do not always know what is going on, although you may feel that this should be one of their responsibilities. This particular tragedy has led some parents to hire medical experts to examine the medical reports that have been sent to them, or to seek out specialists who can examine the children themselves.

Health Insurance

If you are covered by your employer's health plan, your adoptive child will probably be, too, but you must double-check on the procedure to get coverage and find out if it is in any way retroactive. Prior to completing the adoption of my child, I inquired about coverage. My employer said that the coverage would begin immediately upon receipt of adoption papers. However, I knew that I might be taking my daughter for her

---

[1] *The New York Times,* July 13, 1996.

first checkup before I was able to send the papers to my employer since I would be on leave. I then called my insurer. I was advised that I would probably have to pay initial medical fees up front but could claim reimbursement once my papers were filed.

A public school teacher whom I know did not have such luck. She was unable to get retroactive reimbursement for the initial medical fees for her child's care soon after her arrival in the United States, which included relatively common, but expensive, treatment for rashes and a parasite. So find out in advance what you *can* do so that you and your child don't lose out.

2. ADOPTIVE POST-PLACEMENT

Many agencies will require post-placement follow-up reports after your adoption, and also offer counseling and seminars. Post-placement reports may be mandated by the government agency in charge of adoption in the host country, and will be sent there for its records. Requirements will differ, and you should make sure you know what yours are. For my adoption from China, I am required to send a photograph of my daughter twice a year for the next two years. My agency spelled this out in the papers I received with my referral information, but I was not required to do a post-placement report. However, Patti and Pete told me that the authorities in Vietnam have asked for annual photographs of their sons until they turn eighteen!

Don't think that once you are home, you are on your own. Required or not, post-placement reports and services are important. As new parents of children from new surroundings, you may find that your child reacts to his or her environment in ways far different from what your baby-care or child-care books predict, or from what you expect. Flavors, sounds, textures, light, and physical contact will be new experiences for your child, even though you will have had an introductory time together when you went overseas. The adaptation may take a while.

You will feel at times as though you have had your child for years when it is only weeks. There will be moments when it feels as though your child is still brand-new to you. Don't be alarmed by the strange feelings you may sometimes have; that is a function of new parenting in general. And you can use post-placement services as a guide and reinforcement for what you are trying to do.

You may find the post-placement reports to be an imposition. But they also serve as goodwill to your child's birth country. Make sure you fulfill your obligation here. It will pave a smoother way for other parents seeking to adopt there.

3. GETTING A SOCIAL SECURITY NUMBER
FOR YOUR CHILD

It is important to get a social security number for your child for a variety of administrative purposes. For example, you cannot open a bank account in your child's name without one. To obtain a number, go to your local social security office with your child's adoption papers and Green Card, as well as one photo ID of yourself (passport or driver's license), or two IDs if you don't have a photo ID. (Those of us who have traveled probably have several by now.)

You do *not* have to bring your child. The application will be processed in two to three weeks. Call (800)772-1213 for the location of your nearest office.

4. READOPTING YOUR CHILD

You may choose to readopt your child in the United States after you have finished the adoption procedures abroad; or you may be required to do it if your child has been escorted to the United States by a representative of your agency or if just one parent went overseas to do the adoption. A readoption enables you to obtain a U.S. birth certificate for your child. This is a legal proceeding, *but you don't need a lawyer.* Get advice either from your agency, adoption support group, or a local adoption expert if you worked with an out-of-state agency to find out how to go about it in your state. The expense of a readoption involves filing fees and court costs and is likely to be under $200.

As already mentioned, at this writing, the $5,000 tax credit to assist with adoption expenses had been approved only by the U.S. House of Representatives, and a vote by the U.S. Senate is pending. This tax credit was to take effect on January 1, 1997. Adoptive parents will be allowed to spread out the tax credit over several years once an adoption has been completed, but the language of the legislation is unclear about what is meant by a "completed" adoption. Also, international adoptions will be covered by the credit, but until the end of the year 2000.

5. NATURALIZING YOUR CHILD

At some point, you will want to obtain U.S. citizenship for your child. An obvious key advantage is that you will be able to get him or her a U.S. passport. If you plan to travel with your child, this can be important in case the country of birth has travel restrictions. You should do this before the age of eighteen. You do *not* need the services of lawyer.

Obtaining citizenship means working again with INS. You have two options:

1. Obtain Naturalization Form N-400 from INS and then arrange for your child to be interviewed and undergo an oath of allegiance ceremony in the federal district court in your region. You pay $95 and must file two color photos with the form. Instructions on how the photos should appear (similar to passport format) will come with the application. The oath process may be more suitable for an older child; sometimes several hundred new citizens are sworn in at the same time. Processing can take several months.

2. Obtain Form N-643, Application for Certificate of Citizenship on Behalf of an Adopted Child. This is an administrative procedure that requires an interview but no oath of allegiance. Parents must be U.S. citizens, and the process is only done at major INS offices within the area that has jurisdiction for your place of residence. The filing fee was $80 at this writing. You will also need three color photos of your child, a copy of your child's birth certificate, adoption decree, passport from your child's country of origin, and green card, and, if applicable, marriage license and divorce decree of the adoptive parents. (The green card, which comes in the mail after the adoption is completed and a visa has been issued, that is, when the INS procedure and the I-600A have been approved, will be confiscated; you can keep the passport for your child's "life book." One mother I know felt that the green card, which is not really green, was such an important part of her daughter's biography that she had a copy made and laminated for her daughter's life book.) The interview itself usually takes just fifteen minutes. From first request for forms until finalization, the process may take between nine months and one year.

I have most often seen references to the certificate process (N-643). You can request either form from your local INS office or by calling toll-free at (800)870-3676.

PART II

A New Beginning

Issues and Experiences of
International Adoption

8

Becoming a Multicultural Family

In the chapters that follow, I explore many of the issues involved with raising children who were adopted internationally, including cultural questions, raising older children, adopting siblings, and so forth. The information is drawn principally from interviews with adoptive families as well as from seminars and published research.

One of the biggest bridges you will cross as parents of children born in another country is the cultural one. As one writer on adoption has put it, it's not just your child who will make the transition to a new culture, but you, too. I tell people that I have a "kosher Chinese" daughter. I guess I'm her "kosher Chinese" mom.

Yes, an international adoption really *is* different from a domestic one—and I'm not just talking about the paperwork you must do. For when you embark on the process of adopting a child from another country, you are not only taking him or her into your life and culture and out of the one he or she was born in, but putting yourself into your child's. A woman I know says that when people ask her if her child was adopted, she says, *"We were adopted,"* meaning that both she and her child have each journeyed toward a midpoint where they now share common experiences.

To me, one of the wonderful things about international adoption is the opportunity it offers to create an enriched family experience that my friends who have not adopted internationally will never know. I consider it a gift. But it also raises many questions.

For this section of the book, I have taken a lot of the questions that I have been asking myself—and others—and have heard other people discuss. I've provided answers drawn from the many interviews that I have done. These answers obviously reflect the experiences only of those people and your experiences may be altogether different. But I have come upon many common threads in the conversations I have had and believe they can help you.

Dealing with Differences, Especially If Your Child Will Never Look Like You

Irene, whom I mentioned in the section on using facilitators, felt strongly about adopting a child she would feel a common bond with. This meant adopting a European-looking child, preferably one with a Jewish background, if at all possible. As an older single woman, however, many options were not available to her. So she worked with a facilitator who helped her adopt in Paraguay. Irene teaches English as a second language and speaks Spanish fluently; she has spent many of her summers in Central and South America. Her daughter is light-skinned, though Irene does not know her actual background. She has since acknowledged that her daughter is probably partly Guarani. Although this may have been a concern earlier on, she is so bonded to her daughter that now this is inconsequential.

Ruth, a teacher, married a man from Eastern Europe who

already had grown children from a previous marriage. When their attempts to have a biological child failed, he agreed to an adoption, but only if the child was also East European. They adopted a girl from Romania.

Some adopting parents who may have originally tried a domestic adoption and very much want a Caucasian child may choose to adopt from Eastern Europe because they think the children will be blond and fair. But in some areas of Eastern Europe, the children may turn out to be olive-skinned or swarthy. I have heard this about Bulgarian, Hungarian, and Moldovan adoptions. (The owner of an agency that places Hungarian children with families said that about 80 percent of the children are of Gypsy parentage.) If this matters to you, then get as much information as you can about placements in these countries.

Adopting a child who looks completely unlike me—except for our hair color!—did bother me at first. When I was counseled to consider adopting from China, I felt very confused. I had never thought about raising an Asian child. My concern and befuddlement arose, I found, from emotions that I later learned were fundamental to the experience of many people undertaking foreign adoptions. My child would *never* look even a little bit like me—she would certainly not have my blue eyes—and this reality compounded the disappointment I felt about not having had a biological child.

I ultimately came to terms with the dilemma when I met families that had done Asian adoptions years earlier. I attended seminars in which foreign-born adult adoptees described their own experiences and perspectives. The networking and the insights of the adopted young adults helped enormously. So did several excellent books on the subject.

I was particularly moved by the account of Jane, a twenty-five-year-old Korean-born woman of exceptional poise who was adopted at age four and raised in a family that had six Korean-born daughters altogether. Speaking at a panel with three other

Korean-born adoptees, she was very reassuring. "You'll be surprised how attached your children will become to you," she said to a packed seminar of current and expecting parents of Chinese adopted daughters. "Don't worry." Her story brought many of us to tears. It also allayed the anxieties we had about how well our children would accept us. Jane's own experiences have included a search for her parents and a trip back to Korea to see the orphanage where she spent the early part of her life. This was an important step in her journey to herself, but she has never felt less than 100 percent American and her adoptive parents' daughter. She has faced challenges by Korean-born friends she met in high school and college and has learned to deal with these. It has not been easy.

After I'd absorbed the fact that I was going to adopt from China, I began preparing for the change in my life. The summer before, I took an introductory course in Mandarin at the China Institute in New York City and encountered one of the most wonderful teachers I have ever had: Ben Wang. I later took a course from him on Chinese poetry in translation. I didn't then, and still don't, expect to become fluent in Chinese. But I wanted to understand more about how the Chinese language works and to get used to its sounds. Studying with Ben also helped raise my comfort level with the Chinese culture.

Dealing with Religious and Community Differences

But there was another issue bothering me. I am not a very observant Jew, but I consider myself a very "cultural" Jew, and Jewish cultural life has provided a wonderful frame of reference for me and a sense of history and rootedness. My daughter certainly wouldn't look Jewish, and I worried how she would cope with this.

But I realized also that she would not be alone. In my community, there are quite a few international adoptions in Jewish families, so the "Jewish look" is undergoing a transformation. In addition, when I have met adult adoptees from other countries, I find them to be so Americanized that I don't think of them at first as Korean or Colombian or whatever—they are American! Also the American lifestyle—clothing and nutrition, among other things—influences the way that people physically develop and carry themselves. Ultimately, from what I have seen, your children take on a lot of your mannerisms, and will come to seem more like you than you realize.

A funny story from a friend of mine concerned the Korean-born daughter of a friend of *hers* who was preparing to be Bat Mitzvahed. The mother and daughter were chatting about the guest list when the daughter blurted out to her mom that she didn't want a particular yenta to come to the party.

To deal with the reservations I had about China—which were more the result of unfamiliarity than anything else—besides taking Mandarin courses and making more efforts to discuss my plans with people I knew of Chinese background, I also joined Families with Children from China, where I came to know many families in my situation. I found people there to be welcoming and easy to talk to. When I told members of the women's division at the China Institute of my plan during a Chinese New Year dinner, they clucked with pleasure and congratulated me, and invited me to bring my daughter the next year. I felt right at home.

For the children, there are issues, too. How does a child of clearly Asian background explain why his or her first name is Sean or Alison and his last name is Ferguson, Feldman, or Ferrone? I think I'd be more concerned if I were raising my child in a fairly homogeneous community in which she would stand out. But I'd find ways to make sure my child knows about her birth culture and also look for ways for her to share it with her friends and the community.

Some parents give their children first names or middle names that reflect their country of birth. I named my daughter after my grandmother but gave her a Chinese middle name. A number of parents of older adopted children said that they never doubted that they would keep their children's given names, although they may have slightly anglicized them for pronunciation purposes.

Bringing Your Child's Culture into Your Home

The need to get information doesn't stop when your adoption is complete. In fact, becoming a good adoptive parent, like any type of parenting, is a continuous learning process. Fortunately, there are lots of resources available. For instance, I attended seminars that featured adult adoptees who were born in Latin America and Asia and raised in Caucasian families whose backgrounds were mainly European. By listening to what other people had to say—and most important, the adoptees themselves—I picked up some key pointers along the way.

One of the most memorable of many wonderful and wistful comments I have heard to describe the special experience of international adoption came from a woman who, like me, adopted from China. This is how she put it: "My daughter was born in China and is an adopted American. I was born in America and I'm an adopted Chinese."

Indeed, once you adopt "interculturally" (or whatever word you want to use), your child's culture becomes as much a part of you as yours becomes a part of your child's life. At least, that's how it should be.

Judi, mother of three children born in India and a daughter born in China as well as a biological son, knows a family in her community that adopted children from India but has not added anything culturally Indian to the family life. Judi is critical of families who omit their children's birth heritage from their U.S. lives. "They need to get a positive self-image," she says. "They get it from knowing more about where they came from." In the college town she lives in, her family is involved with local Indian and Chinese communities.

I also joined the support group Families with Children from China, which organizes Chinese-centered cultural events for its members. FCC also holds occasional seminars that have included panels of adult Korean adoptees and the parents of adopted Korean children now in their teens.

Don't *impose* your child's birth culture on him or her. At one of the seminars I attended, a Korean-born teenager noted, "My mother is more interested in Korea than I am. My parents enrolled us in Korean school for lessons at one time, but I hated it. I went kicking and screaming, so they stopped."

But scanning America Online, I came across this posting: "We live in a community with very few minorities. I often joke that our Korean kids are the local minority group. We have been extremely fortunate in finding cultural ties with Korea for our nine-year-old daughter who came as an infant. For years we had been eating at an Oriental (not specifically Korean) restaurant where we had met a waitress who was from Korea. This past year she decided to offer Korean language and culture lessons for the Korean adopted kids and her own two part-Korean children. Our daughter loves it. Our older son, however, who is now fifteen and came at the age of eight, wants no part of it."

Do, however, make sure that your child has access to information about the country and culture where he or she was born. You will probably find yourself doing this as part of the adoption anyway, particularly if you travel to get your child. Toys, books, photographs, and art objects are a nice way to decorate your house, to show that you care about your child's roots. Also, as I suggested earlier, you may want to put together a scrapbook, or a life book, of your earliest experiences with your child, including, if you traveled, photographs of the town and, if possible, the orphanage where your child stayed. You may not want to show them to your child right away, but he or she may ask for them.

Also, collect as many artifacts (and your own memories) as you have of your child's early life and record them to serve as your child's point of reference when he or she seeks more information about origins and being adopted.

A number of companies produce ready-made adoption life books (see Appendix), or you can create your own. Throw nothing out! Your son or daughter may treasure the airplane boarding passes, receipts, newspapers, and other artifacts that you obtained in your child's country of birth if you traveled to get him or her. These memories can later be shared with friends and schoolmates and can be part of a family tree project. Instead of your child feeling left out because of his or her different background, the life book and the artifacts you have saved will make him or her feel special.

Eileen and Jerry, whom we met in Chapter 2, adopted two children in Romania born to the same mother, who came from a poor town. Their son, Eli, was very sickly, and this was evident in early photographs of him. There was no certainty, in fact, that he would survive. Eileen won't let Eli see these pictures now, but she is saving them for when he is older. She feels he may want to know about his earliest days in Romania, and Eileen will want to tell him the truth. She has been this way all along. (She also has Romanian dolls and other Romanian crafts in the house to remind her children of their birth country.)

The parents of Korean-born Jane, who adopted several other children from Korea, prepared a photo scrapbook of the orphanage where their children had spent their early years. "It was disgusting," she says, "but when my sisters looked at pictures of it, they didn't see the grime, but all of their old friends. These were their earliest memories."

Encourage your child to include his or her birth roots and current family story in any autobiography he or she might be asked to write for school. Make it a natural part of your family tree.

Raj Badeau, the twelve-year-old son of Sue and Hector

Badeau, gave me a copy of a school report he wrote about India, using his home computer (the "Badeau Press") to produce it. This is not his first publication, he notes on the cover page. That was *My Ten and ¹/₂ Years: Philadelphia, Barre, Montpelier, Cabot, Northampton, Conway, and Calcutta.* His author blurb following the text reads: "Hi, my name is Raj Ashish Badeau. I have nineteen brothers and sisters and two parents. I live in Philadelphia. I'm adopted from Calcutta, India. Also, seventeen of my brothers and sisters are adopted, while two are not. I've written a book before about my family and me. I was ten and a half years old then. Since then I had gotten one new brother and might get another one. Plus a lot has changed. This book is about 'INDIA' where I was born and came from. That's why I am writing a book about it!"

You might occasionally prepare meals based on recipes from your child's birth country—if it's something that you actually enjoy doing yourself. This is part of the meal routine with Raj Badeau's family. Mealtime in the Badeau household—which now includes about fifteen children, since a number of them are grown and on their own, and frequent guests—is organized around regularly rotating menus that feature Latin American and Indian dishes as well as more traditional American food. The intent is to emphasize the diversity of food tastes that are inexpensive and can be prepared in quantity and to reflect the fact that some of their children come from different ethnic backgrounds. Everyone who is able to undertakes different tasks, whether it's helping to shop, cook, serve food, set the table, or clean up.

Culture Days and Culture Camps

Culture days and culture camps give children born in other countries the opportunity to learn about their background in an enjoyable, nonstressful way, and also to see other children who look like them and be able to share their experiences. Some agencies and support groups sponsor such camps, and sometimes groups of parents organize smaller cultural events near where they live. A growing number of books are available that target the concerns of adopted children born outside the United States (see Appendix).

"My culture-camp friendships have lasted for years," says a Korean-born woman in her early twenties, whom I heard speak at a seminar. "I don't feel as comfortable among traditional Koreans."

Preparing for Unkind Comments

Anticipate the possibility that your child or children may encounter racist reactions as they grow up, and be prepared to support your child with good answers and resources. Also think of how to educate your child's classmates in a positive way—as well as adults, including family members, neighbors, friends, and colleagues at work—when they make thoughtless comments. I have heard about remarks on this subject from many adoptive parents and from adult adoptees.

A teenage Korean-born girl raised in a small Minnesota town described how, when she was younger, her classmates teased her about her eyes. As she entered junior high school, the remarks got more severe, particularly regarding sexuality and stereotypes about Asian women. She also was aware of being served last at stores and sometimes seated in the back of her classroom. These experiences hurt, but her supportive mother has made sure always to be there for her and to make her realize that the problem isn't hers but that of whoever has targeted her. In communities where your child might be the only "different" person, participation in a culture camp can be particularly valuable.

The Double Dilemma of an Adopted Youngster

For Jose Badeau, who was eighteen when I wrote this, the journey to learn more about his roots was quiet and private. Adopted at age two from El Salvador, he spent much of his youth in Vermont, where he was the only ethnic child in a white community. He felt much more comfortable when his family moved to a racially mixed suburb of Philadelphia, where his schoolmates included Hispanic people. "In Vermont, people sometimes called me 'nigger.' Here, the only time I was called that was by Spanish-speaking students who looked at me curiously because I wasn't doing too well in Spanish," he says. His parents, Hector and Sue, and his brothers and sisters are always there to provide support, but certain problems are specific to him, and he must try to solve them in his own way.

This is not an uncommon situation for adopted children, and it is an issue that we as parents must learn to accept. We can be there, but, as Hector says, must not impose. Similarly, while Raj became interested in learning about India, Jose for years expressed no interest in his Latin American roots. Hector one day noticed that Jose was surfing on the Internet and reading a Web page about Mayan Indians. He was happy about that but didn't say anything. He realized that Jose was taking a very private journey.

A challenge the Badeau family sometimes faces is the perception that some of the children are there temporarily. "When we moved in, some kids came over from next door and asked about us," Hector told me. "I said they're mine, they're adopted. One kid yelled back, loud enough for a lot of people to hear, 'I *told* you, Mom, they're *not* foster kids, they're *good* kids.'" The very embarrassed mother came by later, introduced herself and also apologized. Without trying hard, the Badeaus are a lesson in human relations.

Having so many children, including several who have physical disabilities, means that the siblings provide mutual support.

There's a high energy level in the house, and at times things are intense. Yet, says Sue, "In a big family setting, the children often absorb each other's energy." In small families, she notes, the parents often get the brunt of it.

There is also a strong encouragement of individuality, which can be an interesting lesson for a blended family of adopted and biological children. On the walls of the dining room are family photos. Sue has meticulously organized a photo collage of each child in the household, including those who have grown and gone on to form their own families. (Sue and Hector already have grandchildren, since they adopted two groups of older siblings—five in one case, six in another—and some of those children are now in their twenties.) The collage is made up of graduation photos, pictures of awards and other special events or family gatherings, all with neat, handwritten captions. Similar pictures show Sue and Hector when they were much younger, too.

I came away from a visit with the Badeaus feeling something that I know I shouldn't—awe. But this is the life they have chosen, and they're doing it well. Yet Sue reflected with some wonder at the challenge I was taking on as a single parent. "I don't know how people can adopt on their own. Hector and I are a real team—partners—and have a mind frame to take one day at a time and not blow things up into huge crises."

Developing a Thick Skin

Some comments can truly hurt. It helps to inculcate your children with a strong sense of self-esteem. At a panel discussion of young adults adopted from Colombia, a woman now in college who was raised as a Jew described the discomfort of a boyfriend's parents at meeting her, since she clearly looked different (and not European Jewish): olive-skinned and possibly of native Indian background. He eventually broke up with her. Her reaction was that the racism was his problem as much as his parents' and that he was not someone worth getting serious about, so she moved on.

A young man on the same panel, also raised as a Jew and now attending law school, quipped: "It's great being adopted. When you fill in your law school application, you can check two boxes: Hispanic *and* Jewish, and you'll have a much easier time getting in!" True or not, a sense of humor is a good device to move beyond the hurt.

An adult Korean adoptee comments that people sometimes say to her with surprise, "You speak English so well!"

Be Candid About Your Child's Origins

Be open about your child's cultural background if he or she asks for it. If you can afford to do so, plan to take a trip with your child to his or her birth country when your child is old enough.

For many years, Judi's daughter Rehema, who was adopted from India at the age of seven, talked about wanting to visit her first home, and Judi promised that when Rehema reached the tenth grade they would go. Joined by two Indian friends, they made the trip in 1995, visiting the two orphanages in Calcutta where Rehema had lived after an uncle abandoned her. In one of these she had been badly neglected. She found the sight of the orphanage drab and lonely. Gazing into the courtyard, Rehema saw children wandering aimlessly. It was clearly an intense experience, Judi recounts, and Rehema remained silent. Yet, Judi says, the trip not only restored some of Rehema's "Indian-ness" to her but also underscored how, over the years, Rehema had become a "sophisticated American."

Share Your Background with Your Child

Do share your background and roots with your child. Your child is part of your family and will grow up with your name and your traditions, and very likely will pick up your quirks and your accent. Just because your child comes from a Catholic country and was probably born to a Catholic mother does not mean he or she should be raised as a Catholic. My Chinese-born daughter is Jewish, like me. She is part of everything that I do and hold dear to my own life. By the same token, I take part in Chinese-focused activities such as Chinese New Year celebrations. As much as my daughter has become part of my birth culture, I am becoming part of hers, too.

Be Yourself

Don't confuse your child! Be who you are: the child's parent and role model. You (parent *and* child) are now part of a special, unique family. Be yourselves. Don't deny your culture and don't deny his or hers. Celebrate who you each are.

During my home-study interview, when I had decided to adopt from China, I was asked what my thoughts were about how I would raise my child. "Well," I said, "I live near a university that has a large East Asian studies program, and I'm thinking of looking for a baby-sitter from China or someone who speaks Chinese who can raise my child to know about Chinese things." My social worker said this was absolutely the wrong way to choose a baby-sitter. Above all, she said, I needed to find someone who loved children and was experienced with them. The cultural emphasis might be confusing—to me *and* the child. This was one of the best pieces of advice I got, and, fortunately, I got it early on. This isn't to say that my child won't be exposed to her roots. Considering the high number of Chinese adopted girls in my neighborhood, she is bound to know them. But I want her to understand that she is my daughter above all and not to feel that her loyalties must be divided.

Adopted children who do not resemble their adoptive parents will experience their "different-ness" in different ways. I was saddened to hear a Korean adoptive teenager describe the identity crisis that many Korean adoptees she grew up with went through. Some were suicidal, she said, and "did lots of unhealthy things." She got through, she thinks, because her parents were "very open about it all the time."

Another young man said that he never experienced an identity crisis. "You know you're growing up in a Caucasian U.S. family," he said. "Being adopted is part of your identification, and a way to feel special. Culture days helped me to appreciate that there are other people in my situation. When you're adopted, you're able to see things through two perspectives; adoption gives you a neat perspective!"

Finding Support Group Resources

I have benefited from the resources provided by Families with Children from China. Enough children had been adopted by 1996 for my FCC chapter to sponsor a full-day cultural celebration, which more than a hundred families attended. It included arts and crafts, music, puppet shows, a musical presentation, Chinese food, games and recreation, sales of Chinese-made toys and clothing, and, at the end of the day, a parade of children and their families, grouped according to the town they were from.

There are dozens of cultural support groups and newsletters that exist for families with children adopted from outside of the United States. The National Adoption Information Clearinghouse will send you a list of adoption support groups in your state (see Appendix).

9

New Adoptive Families

One of the exciting trends in international adoption is that more of us who had dreamed of becoming parents, and didn't think we ever would, now can. Adoption is increasingly open to single applicants. Older single people and couples may also adopt, though they many not be able to adopt newborns. More and more lesbian and gay couples are adopting children internationally, but it is a tricky subject to discuss for reasons I'll mention later. And adoption organizations and agencies are encouraging families to reach out for children around the world who have special needs, such as basic surgical procedures, that, in many instances, can be attended to easily in the United States but not in their home countries.

The Special Challenge of Being a Single Adoptive Parent

So many single people are adopting children nowadays that it is no longer difficult to find resources. The needs and concerns of

116

single parents of any type are compelling, and our numbers are growing. But single or married, straight or gay, parents work hard and raising a child is expensive. For single parents who are adopting, the pressures can be extra intense. We know why we're adopting, and many of us have done research and homework to prepare ourselves.

Many of us also feel more in control of our lives by making the proactive decision to adopt. But it's one thing to prepare for it and quite another when your child and you are a family at last. The easygoing rhythms of single life will have to be shelved for quite a while. Though one form of anticipation is over, another form—and a new relationship—is just beginning and due to last a lifetime.

Building a Support System

A support system is one of the first things you will need and should begin to identify and create before you adopt. If there isn't a single parents' support group in your community, you might try to form one. Sometimes the type of adoption you do may lend itself to such a system. By adopting from China, I already had a large support system, because in my neighborhood there were already quite a few single moms of Chinese-born children. There are also quite a few single parent networks that sponsor seminars and organize play groups and child-care co-ops.

As single parents, we sometimes want to assert our independence. After all, we have made the bold decision to adopt on our own. But there are times when we'll have to surrender a bit and admit that we also need help. Offers of free baby-sitting, hand-me-downs, a home-cooked meal, and all sorts of other gifts should be welcomed by single parents without either feeling guilty or obliged to give in return. The principle here, I think, is that when we are able to do so, we *will* give back.

When my friend Irene was in the throes of doing her adoption and feeling desolate and lonely, her friends rallied around her. Three showers were held for her, and Helen has a closet packed with clothes. Irene says: "I don't think I've spent fifty dollars on clothes." Since the adoption, one friend has made a point of offering free baby-sitting two or three times a month to give Irene a physical and psychological break. And while I was still waiting, Irene invited me over to scour through clothing, toys, and books that her daughter, Helen, had outgrown. My own closet was well stocked long before my adoption had taken place.

Here are a few things to think about if you adopt on your own:

- Do you have a flexible work situation? If not, can you think of a way to make it so and propose it to your employer?
- Do you have a backup plan besides your regular child care if you or your child becomes ill? We have to face the fact that as single parents, we have a particular worry if something happens to us. (I bought a beeper.)

Marlene had always planned to adopt a child if she hadn't married and started a biological family. So early on she established her own business in order to be self-sufficient and capable of being fully in charge of her own child's care, and allowing her to be with her child for as long as necessary. When we spoke, she had received a referral from China and was waiting for news that she could go. Although her daughter would stay with her for the early part of her life, Marlene had already put her name on a day-care waiting list.

Have you mapped out a child-care plan yet? Have you explored the possibility of shared child-care and baby-sitting exchanges to give friends a few hours of your time in exchange for theirs so you can be freed up? At the recommendation of another single mom, I put the word out to the superintendent of the apartment building I live in that I would be looking for child care at some point. The super often knows networks of baby-sitters who work in the building and can help. I wanted to find a baby-sitter who did not have to travel far to get to my home and ended up hiring the adult daughter of an older woman who had been working for many years with another family in my building. This was good for everyone. She had impeccable references. She knew the family and the building, and we hit it off. I also knew that if anything happened to her, her mother could come in. And my neighbor and I agreed that we could also piggyback our child care at times. Her son was six months older than my daughter.

If you're not set on adopting an infant, then perhaps you might consider adopting an older child. "When I saw single mothers struggling with their babies because there was no father to share the work, I knew I couldn't handle it," says Alice, who adopted eight-year-old Nadia from Russia (see below).

The Special Needs of Single Adoptive Parents

Parenting alone is already a challenge. Adopting alone presents more hurdles. The types of responsibilities that couples can share—discipline issues with older children (including, in some instances, dealing with attachment disorder) or shielding your child from potential discrimination or answering questions that sometimes make you feel on the defensive—must be handled entirely by you, with no one there automatically seconding what you're saying or able to share your anguish and occasional grief at the actions of others that hurt you or your child. And, as any other single parent faces, you may have to make quick decisions or face emergencies without a backup system.

One approach is to create your own backup. Adoptive parents speak a special language of common experience, and it makes a huge difference to have them accessible to you. My friend Irene initiated a single parents' group in her synagogue.

Ten parents came to the first meeting, of those, three were single fathers through divorce and three were single mothers of adopted children. Although Irene does not want to restrict her social circle to single parents, she recognizes that single parents have specific concerns that couples do not: the loneliness and tension of being the sole parent, particularly if your child is ill or acting out; specific financial pressures as the sole breadwinner; and, particularly, days when the pressure of single parenting seem to boil over. Irene reached such a day—a week, really—about three months after she had brought Helen home. There had been a record-breaking blizzard, and for three days they didn't go out. The stress was relentless. The support of friends, especially other single adoptive mothers whom she spoke to by phone, kept her going and gave her relief. The singles' group will arrange occasional dinners and holiday events—often a lonely time in the year—when everyone can be together.

Also, other single parents understand and empathize with Irene's challenges. They love being parents—"My life is so much more interesting now, I have so much more joy," Irene says—but it's difficult. Irene finds it especially grating when married friends say, "I don't know how you do it." "I do it—*we* do it—and we don't have to be reminded of this all the time," Irene says. With other singles, there's a good deal more sharing of similar issues.

I also participate in a single mothers' group through Families with Children from China. We have monthly meetings which double as play dates for our daughters.

Giving Yourself Private Time

One of the most difficult issues for single parents is the incessant demand on their time, especially if they work full-time. Several months after she brought Helen home, Irene realized that the stress of working and child care, with no break, was too much for her. A teacher, she was always home almost an hour before her baby-sitter's eight-hour day was over. Irene decided to keep that hour for herself. After she finishes teaching, she comes back to her neighborhood, buys a newspaper, and goes to a local café to relax and read before returning home. It is only an hour, but it is precious private time, and it puts her in a better frame of mind to take care of Helen.

I have found that new motherhood in my forties has been an invigorating time for me. I feel a lot younger somehow. When I'm in my fifties, my daughter will be in school, and I will be enjoying her experiences. My other single friends who have adopted say the same thing. "I don't worry about old age anymore," says Irene, at forty-eight the mother of two-year-old Helen. At a friend's suggestion, she was getting ready to enter Helen in a peewee race and dreamed of sharing her first Mother's Day with Helen—something that she had longed for for many years. (See Appendix for books on single parenting.)

Gay and Lesbian Adoptive Households

Adoption has become an increasingly acceptable option to gay and lesbian couples who wish to have a family. According to Wayne Steinman, a gay parent in New York City, international adoption is often easier to do than in the United States because of antigay bias in the organizations handling adoptions in this country. "As long as you have the money and you're working with a cooperative social worker, international adoption is easier," he told me. Steinman is a leading advocate of gay and lesbian adoption, and has compiled information resources on agencies, organizations, adoption attorneys, social workers, as well as other types of information to help gay and lesbian parents complete successful adoptions (see Appendix).

Among adoption professionals, there is some reluctance to deal directly with gay and lesbian households that wish to adopt. Virtually no country has a progay policy, and, as a result, openly gay and lesbian couples are discouraged from adopting. "You never come out in a home study," says Steinman. Paradoxically, this situation can present a problem to social workers or agencies when preparing home studies since such deliberate closeting does not honestly describe the household in which the adopted child will be raised. And adoption professionals whom I have spoken to, who believe that gay and lesbian couples are eminently qualified to be adoptive parents, are themselves ambivalent about preparing a home study that is not entirely truthful. One social worker I spoke to had done home studies for gay and lesbian couples in the past but had more recently become nervous, she said, because she feared that she could lose her license if it were discovered that she had misrepresented a household. Even International Concerns for Children, which energetically advocates for the placement of as many institutionalized children as possible, is rather coy about gay and lesbian couples. Its comprehensive and invaluable *Report on Intercountry Adoption*, which seems to cover just about every topic imaginable, discusses gay parenting in an oblique manner, reserving a portion of a page to what it terms alternative families. Presumably, gay parents can refer to ICC's many references to resources for single parents when researching adoption options.

Steinman and his partner, who adopted in the United States in the mid-1980s, did so as an openly gay couple, and they confronted many problems in the process. After they had been certified to adopt, and after they had expressed a willingness to adopt a special-needs child, they went through twenty-four applications and were turned down twenty-four times. Finally, they received a referral for an autistic boy, and rejected the referral. "We knew that we had the right to say no," Steinman says. "And we urge lesbian and gay couples to take that stand as well." They subsequently got a referral for an infant girl born to a drug-addicted mother. Although their daughter had drugs in her system at the time, she is now a healthy nine-year-old.

Gay and lesbian couples have found most opportunities to adopt internationally either in China or Russia, and occasionally, in Brazil. Countries that accept only married heterosexual couples are obviously off-limits (to straight single parents as well). Once the adoption takes place, Steinman encourages gay and lesbian families to be open. Once the parenting begins, adoptive families may encounter some of the same awkward reactions from strangers who see a same-sex couple with an obviously foreign child that straight couples get, perhaps compounded by a dose of homophobia. It is still a new issue in the adoption community, and a certain amount of discomfort prevails when discussing it.

But more is being written, including a *New York Times* article that appeared on May 16, 1996. From my point of view, as a single parent, a gay couple has an edge over me because there are two parents. Furthermore, there are good support systems, especially in large cities, for gay and lesbian families.

Adopting an Older Child

One of the recent phenomena of adoption is the growing number of older single and married people seeking to form or expand their families. Agencies that used to cap applicants' age at the mid-thirties now accept parents who are quite a bit older. This trend falls into line with a more general trend of later marriage, consequent infertility in older couples, and healthier lifestyles leading to longer lives. Some older (40+) would-be parents want infants, but some countries have an age cap for babies.

These parents may want to consider adopting an older child; many countries have such children legally available for adoption, and sometimes the fee is lower than for a much younger child. (In this context, "older" means at least two years old.) So if you're a bit older than the average parent and are not interested in an infant, this may well be the right option for you—and a good option, as well, if you want to adopt fairly quickly.

An excellent source of information on older children is the photo-listing resource provided by International Concerns for

Children. It contains listings on hundreds of older children available for adoption, including the agencies that are trying to place them and their fees. Some of these children also have health or learning disabilities, and the listings describe these as well as the possible availability of financial aid if you're interested in such an adoption.

Here are some reasons that might lead you to consider adopting an older child:

• You are single and don't have the energy to raise an infant, yet you very much want to be a parent.

• You live in a community, such as a university town or diverse urban area, where there is a good support system for an older child who speaks a different language and might experience a form of culture shock when coming to the United States.

• You have raised other children who are now grown and would welcome a somewhat older child into your house.

• You are an older parent/couple who prefers not to have an enormous age gap between you and your child and also don't know if you have the stamina to raise an infant.

AVA, BOB, AND TIM

For a number of years, Ava and Bob, journalists now in their mid-forties, lived and worked overseas, and did not have a lifestyle that lent itself to having children. In any case, Bob says, "Up until the point that we decided to have kids, we didn't want them at all." Then, during a visit home, when they were about to turn forty, they saw that many of their friends had started families. "They were really cute," says Ava. Bob picks up, "We realized something was missing." After Ava failed to get pregnant over the next few months and after a brief attempt at fertility treatments, they turned to adoption, in part because treatments were hard to come by where they were living, and they didn't have time.

Also, Bob says, "To me it never really mattered about having a biological kid." Back in the United States, they began investigating domestic and foreign adoptions. The U.S. option did not appeal to them; they did not relish the prospect of a birth mother changing her mind at the last minute. Adopting in Eastern Europe, where they had been working, was now becoming available, and this had an obvious appeal. They focused on Russia; Ava and Bob both speak Russian, and they knew of other couples who had adopted there.

Settling on an agency recommended by someone who had had an excellent experience, Ava and Bob asked for a very young girl. "I love little girl's clothing," Ava once told me. Their agency soon sent them a picture of a little boy who was already two years old. Rather than question the assignment, Bob said, they found that "he became more irresistible by the day." They never asked the agency why this choice was made.

Traveling to Russia was relatively easy for them: they were familiar with it and could speak the language. The orphanage, though understaffed, was far better than Ava and Bob had expected: it was clean and the children were well cared for and well dressed. Most of the children had had minimal exposure to men, so when they first saw Bob, some of them screamed and ran away. But over the two weeks that Ava and Bob spent there, they got to know him and eventually came right to him and started calling him "Papa."

The two weeks also gave Bob and Ava time to get to know their son, whom they named Tim, which is close to his birth name. He "began calling us Mama and Papa in a few days," Ava says. Although Ava and Bob hired Russian-speaking babysitters to watch Tim when he was little, he picked up English quickly and lost most of his Russian. Because he was a somewhat older child who was walking and toilet-trained, Ava was able to resume a fairly active schedule of assignments, some of which required her to travel. Ava and Bob were able to hire live-in help, but they tried to coordinate their assignments so that one parent was always home. On occasion, they took Tim with them.

They experienced the first of two glitches when it came to finalizing the adoption. A young bureaucrat took a long time to approve the adoption because of his concern as to who was actually responsible for Tim's well-being until he reached adulthood. This was a technicality that Ava and Bob resolved by signing an agreement that said they would write regular letters reporting on Tim's well-being. The second came when their agency's principal contact in Russia demanded an extra $1,000 for her services, which Ava and Bob had not been told about nor did they feel was entirely legitimate. They paid it anyway.

A third issue—which Ava and Bob did not personally confront but, they say, other adoptive parents going to Russia have—is whether the child has been fully relinquished. Clarifying this situation can delay an adoption. "There's nothing worse than meeting a child that you think will be your child and then you're told there's a problem," Ava says. She attributes this problem to agencies that don't do their job. "There are really great differences in agencies," she adds. "You get different vibes and some agencies aren't so organized."

Tim's adjustment to his new family went relatively smoothly. Ava and Bob's ability to speak Russian and their familiarity with the culture no doubt made a big difference. They took lots of pictures during their stay, and Tim enjoys looking at pictures of the orphanage, especially of the women who cared for him.

Challenges

There are, however, certain issues to bear in mind when adopting an older child.

• **Language.** It may take longer for an older child to acquire ease and fluency in English. This can have emotional repercussions if the child feels like an outsider anyway, and may lead to acting out and behavior problems.

• **Developmental lag.** It's important to remember that children adopted from overseas come from poor backgrounds, and even if they have been placed with a nurturing foster family, they are still disadvantaged. If they have been in an institution, there are further disadvantages, though this may depend on the quality of care the child received. A seven-year-old who has been abandoned, institutionalized, and then taken from his birthplace to a new country and culture will have to deal with many more social, physical, and emotional changes than a seven-year-old who has lived with the same parent or parents since birth, and may have to contend with developmental difficulties.

John and Denise were forty and fifty years old, respectively, when they adopted two Hungarian-born Gypsy sibling girls, then five and six years old. Abandoned very young, they were placed in an orphanage that then placed them together in a foster household, also a Gypsy family in which the father was absent. The foster mother, who had other children, became very attached to the girls, particularly the younger one, and told them that she was their biological mother.

The sisters are extremely close and remain so three years later. They share almost everything, including a bedroom. Once in the United States, both picked up English quickly and soon lost much of their Hungarian language. But the elder daughter has had difficulty learning to read and both are in special education classes. Denise believes that their cultural background has had a lot to do with it. "There wasn't much learning going on where they were growing up," she says. The foster mother was semiliterate, and neither girl knew how to count to ten in Hungarian by the time they were adopted. And although they have excellent social skills, they are not learning at their age level. The elder daughter is far more disciplined than the younger, who had been babied by her foster mother. Their slowness to learn has been the greatest concern for John and Denise in raising their daughters.

Bonding: Is It Hard with the Older Adopted Child?

Within the adoption community, you are likely to encounter discussion and debate about what is known as attachment disorder and the behavioral problems that may be associated with it. (See also Chapter 5, Health Issues.) This type of problem may arise if a child has been institutionalized over a period of time and has not received the one-on-one attention that enables the child to develop trusting and loving relationships. But it is a controversial topic, too, and I don't believe there's a single answer or a predictable response. The adoption counselor I worked with advised me against adopting an older child for this reason. She had encountered difficulties of this nature as the result of adopting a twenty-eight-month-old girl who had lived in a deprived orphanage environment. Her daughter is now in her early twenties and still has emotional problems related to her earliest years.

If you are considering adopting an older child who has been institutionalized, you might want to seek the advice of a specialist familiar with this issue. You should speak with other adoptive parents who have also done so. Children brought up in stable settings are more likely to be able to bond with you. You should not assume, however, that your child will have this disorder and that it is untreatable. It simply may not be the case, or if it is and you recognize it early on, you can get treatment and therapy.

A Bulgarian Adoption: Dreams for an Infant Turn into the Adoption of a Seven-Year-Old

Louise and Jack, Virginia-based educators in their mid-forties, had set out to adopt an infant, and had turned to international adoption in 1994 after efforts to complete a domestic independent adoption fell through. In the process of checking out different agencies, they saw a photograph of a Bulgarian boy who had just turned seven. "There was an instant connection," said Louise, and the couple contacted the Minnesota-based agency that worked with the orphanage (known in Bulgaria as a kindergarten) where the boy lived. The adoption itself took a long time to complete—this is Louise's main complaint—but once the assignment was approved, Louise and Jack were allowed not only to have regular contact with their son-to-be (including telephone calls and monthly gift packages), but were even permitted to visit him in Bulgaria though the final adoption was still a few months away.

Miklos (his given name which they kept) had been abandoned at the age of four days, and although his parents were unknown, the kindergarten had a health history of him from that time forward.

Louise found the orphanage care givers, who were regarded as well-trained professionals, to be sensitive and welcoming, and the quality of the care high. Miklos had been well prepared for the meeting. Louise and Jack had sent on photographs and videos of themselves and their relatives so that they weren't complete strangers to him. They also met a local couple who had developed an attachment to Miklos and had started setting aside money for him.

When they brought Miklos home, after what Louise calls a honeymoon phase, he entered a period of regular temper tantrums. There was an initial language problem and homesickness. Louise contacted other families who had adopted children from Bulgaria, including some children from his own kindergarten, and they have met for cultural weekends. (The on-line news-groups were helpful in this regard.) Within six months, Miklos was speaking almost fluent English and within eight months it was complete; he was even forgetting some of his Bulgarian. Meanwhile, the orphanage sent him regular letters and gifts.

Louise feels very lucky about Miklos: "He's healthy as a horse but he needed a lot of dental work." At his first medical checkup in the United States, the doctor said that except for a minor parasite problem, Miklos was in excellent physical condition.

The family has bonded well, says Louise, who is trying to organize a Bulgarian culture camp somewhere in their region. Using on-line bulletin boards, she has networked with other families who adopted in Bulgaria.

WHEN ALICE MET NADIA

Part I: Their Meeting in Moscow

I've already told you about Alice. She's the lawyer who, although she had scrupulously researched many agencies and had a few finalists, then chose one when she fell in love with a Russian girl whom she first spotted on videotape. The problems Alice encountered as she sought to adopt an older child and the long waiting period were due to changes in Russian adoption law beyond the power of her agency (see Chapter 5). Alice had to travel to Russia twice to complete the adoption. Having had a very long wait, plus two encounters, she was able to prepare to bring Nadia into her life. And prepare she did.

She describes her first meeting with Nadia as a "wonderful and surreal experience." Nadia had been told the day before that Alice was coming and was prepared; she seemed happy and a bit scared. "Nadia was brought into a reception room where I was waiting and chatting with another family. I held out my arms and she came right to me and wrapped her arms around my neck. I told her in Russian that she was my daughter and that I was her mother. She was very shy and looked down at her feet most of the time. She was very receptive to my Russian and responded to all my questions and endearments. She had no English at all." This first visit, which also included a little dance recital by Nadia's group, lasted about an hour and a half. Then Alice, who had been joined by another adoptive family, had to leave. "It was very hard," she says.

Alice arranged to have this meeting videotaped, and she considers it precious. Once they were home in Florida, she said, Nadia watched the video of the meeting over and over again. Each time, Alice says, she ran to her and said, in Russian, "You said, 'You're my daughter!' You said, 'You're my daughter!'" After the first three weeks, however, she stopped watching it as often. Alice believes that Nadia's repeated viewings were part of her grief process at the loss of her life in Russia and her friends there.

Nadia had been informed about the adoption six months earlier. She had received a family photo album Alice sent. And except for the clothing that Alice gave her the day before she picked Nadia up, the photo album was the only possession that Nadia took from the orphanage. The other clothing and gifts she had sent to Nadia had been "absorbed" by the orphanage. Alice was not surprised.

The following day Alice was allowed to see Nadia for just one hour. This visit took place at her hostess's apartment. A teenage neighbor translated so she could talk in greater depth with Nadia and explain that she would be leaving the next day, but would be returning several weeks later. Although the visit was a good one, Alice was upset by how hungry Nadia seemed to be when lunch was served. "She dropped the candy she was holding and practically dived into the soup," she says. "I hated the idea of leaving this child behind for several weeks, knowing she might not be getting the nutrition she needed."

Part 2: Getting Ready to Leave

After her first trip to Russia in April 1996—a five-day whirl-wind—Alice went home for a few weeks and then returned in mid-May for ten exhausting days. She shared an apartment with another mother using the same agency who was adopting a nine-year-old from the same orphanage. They had their daughters from the third day that they were there, so they then had six days of transition until each headed home.

"The girls were a joy—and a handful—in Moscow," Alice says. "We took them to the Bolshoi Ballet the very first night we had them. We were concerned about this decision, but it turned out to be a good one because their strict orphanage behavior was still in effect and the girls were very well behaved. In fact, they were enthralled!"

Within days, the girls began testing limits. "They started off being little robots. All I had to say was 'Spat?' (sleep, nap) and Nadia would head for the bedroom, take off her outer clothes, and crawl under the covers." Soon, however, both girls had begun to learn the art of whining.

Every new experience was thrilling to them. Within minutes of arriving at the apartment, the girls were running back and forth to each other showing off their new possessions, mostly new clothes. On her second day, Nadia discovered a blouse with the colorful tag still attached. When Alice cut it off, Nadia grabbed the tag and ran to her friend exclaiming, "Mama bought me a picture!"

By her third night with Alice, Nadia began to show a difficult and fragile side. She started crying at bedtime and sobbed for nearly an hour. "I held her and rocked her like a baby," says Alice. "The next day she cuddled in my arms and said 'Mama, I love you. You're my sweetheart.'" Then, while they still had a few days left in Moscow, the girls decided they preferred each other's mother and refused to speak to their own at times.

Part 3: Coming Home

Nadia had her first tantrum on the plane home. Alice had had to wake her up very early to catch the plane. Twenty hours later she was still awake—and fell asleep only twenty minutes before the plane was to land. As Alice woke her up to tighten the seat belt for landing, Nadia became angry and pulled a full-fledged tantrum, complete with sobbing, flailing arms and legs, and beating fists. Her anger lasted all the way through the airport, through customs (she threw raisins in the immigration office and sat on the floor, refusing to move), and onto the connecting flight.

By landing time, however, she had calmed down and was giggling. Alice had found just the trick: she pulled out the photo album she had made for Nadia months earlier and sent to the orphanage with pictures of Alice's family and friends—the people she would soon meet—and also with Polaroids of her friends from the orphanage. "My friends waiting at the gate saw a charming, smiling little girl and a completely exhausted mother," says Alice. "Someone brought her helium balloons, a true delight. She was thrilled with the gifts and attention, but the highlight came when she found a large, opened box of Kleenex in the backseat of my friend's car on the way home. She screeched, 'Mama, boomahgah (paper), boomahgah, boomahgah!' She pulled out pieces of tissue and waved them excitedly at those standing outside the car. When we unloaded the car, the box of Kleenex ended up in Nadia's room among her most prized possessions."

Once home, Nadia finally fell asleep and slept for thirteen hours. The next day she appeared fine, apparently not jet-lagged. And although the next few days were punctuated by a few outbursts, including protests at bedtime, Alice was delighted to have Nadia home with her at last. Even so, there have been behaviors that prompted concern. During one of her tantrums, Nadia spit at Alice. But as the result of reading up on what to expect, Alice wasn't completely surprised.

Adopting an older child often entails communicating across language barriers. Alice prepared by studying Russian for seven months with tapes and a tutor prior to her trip, and felt that this preparation made an enormous difference. "I can't imagine how scary it would be to a child to be delivered to strangers who don't know her language," she says. "I firmly believe that a parent owes it to the child to do everything she/he/they can to make the child feel safe and cared for, including learning how to communicate with that child." As for Nadia, Alice located a summer program where she could take half-day English classes and also found an afternoon day-care program that included two Russian boys her age.

As a single parent, Alice understands well the need to accept help, and her family and friends were wonderful. One friend gave Alice a very special gift: she slept over the night Alice returned so that Alice could get a good night's sleep after twenty hours on the plane.

Learning from Alice's Experience

There are several ways parents can prepare to bring an older adopted child from another country into their homes. Alice recommends the following:

• Reading about adopting older children is essential. Books and articles can be identified by making inquiries on-line or through organizations such as AFA, ICC, and NAIC. (See Appendix for listing.)

• Membership in the Parent Network for Post-Institutionalized Children can be very helpful through its support programs and its newsletter (see Appendix for contact information). Alice believes that it is imperative that any parent considering adopting an older child who has been institutionalized should obtain as much information as possible about its impact on children. This way, parents can be better prepared about types of behaviors to expect and how to respond to them.

• "A support group is essential," Alice says, noting that in her case it is the Russian parenting mailing list on the Internet.

• Learning a fair amount of the child's language is of great importance.

Adopting a Child with Special Needs

Among the many children in overseas institutions who are waiting to be placed with permanent families are those who have disabilities. Some of these may be severe and require lengthy treatment or extensive surgery. Others could involve relatively simple procedures that are readily available in the United States but not in the child's home country.

If you are the type of person who welcomes the challenge of a child with special needs in your life, or if you have access to top medical care for such a child, you might find the prospect of doing such an adoption the right thing for you. You can often get financial assistance to do a special-needs adoption. A number of organizations such as ICC exist explicitly to promote such adoptions, and there is a wealth of information.

If you're resourceful, you'll be surprised at the amount of services available to you, in some cases free of charge. Jerry and Eileen learned that the state of New York, where they were living at the time, had free therapy services for children like their son, Eli, and they obtained immediate assistance to give him physical and speech therapy. Therapists came to their home, which was very convenient, because Jerry, who had recently completed a social work degree, was there much of time and actively participated in the therapy.

Eli is now a talkative, bouncy three-year-old—worlds away from the scrawny, pale, and sickly child whose early hospital photographs Eileen showed me.

Financial Considerations

In some instances, you will be eligible for social-security support if you adopt from overseas, and you may also find that the agency you work with has a scholarship fund or other assistance if you are willing to adopt a disabled child. Judi Kloper, who has adopted four children altogether, three of whom have a disability, notes that an agency in Oregon, for which she now does some work, will provide financial assistance to do a home study for parents willing to undertake special-needs adoptions.

JUDI AND PETER'S STORY

Judi Kloper and Peter Owens wanted to start a family soon after they were married in their early twenties, but after Judi had five miscarriages, they looked seriously at adoption. This was in the early 1980s and they were both twenty-six. They turned to international adoption because they didn't have to wait and race wasn't an issue for them. But their initial experiences in researching foreign adoption were scary, according to Judi. "The agencies sent us photographs of starving, handicapped kids," she said. They then began attending classes on adoption at a community college sponsored by a local adoption agency, and there they met a family with an adopted infant boy from India. Judi and Peter were instantly smitten with the idea of adopting from India, and over the next few years, they undertook three adoptions from that country. Working with one agency in their home state of Oregon, they found the procedure to be very smooth, mainly because the agency had given a detailed description of each step in the process. There were no surprises.

They were warned, however, that there could be problems with children adopted from India, who were often very small. In fact, the first child they adopted, Dana, was eight weeks old and weighed just four pounds when they got him. Over time, Judi and Peter realized that Dana was not developing appropriately. After an extensive checkup, he was diagnosed as having cerebral palsy and hearing loss. Now fourteen years old, Dana is in a wheelchair most often though he can sometimes use a walker. He can understand sign language and speak, but with difficulty; he can't sign because of the CP. "He is totally dependent on other people," Judi says, "but very bright and happy."

Judi was twenty-seven at the time of Dana's diagnosis. "It was sad and I was very upset," she says. "My mom said I would always love him. We took him everywhere with us and got therapy for him and also took out loans against our savings." Judi and Peter did, indeed, fall in love with Dana. Despite his physical disabilities, Dana is mainstreamed at school and has performed very well academically, even studying Spanish. The hardest issue, though, is that classmates who once socialized with Dana when he was younger are tending to reject him now.

When Judi and Peter undertook their next two adoptions from India, each of those children, Chandan and Rehema, also had special needs. Chandan, who was seven when they adopted him, had spent his early years in an institution and was deaf. "We figured we could handle another deaf kid," says Judi, "but we didn't realize that it's difficult to teach language after they're seven or eight. In fact, he had acquired no language skills at all." Chandan also turned out to be autistic. Now nineteen years old, he spends four nights a week in a transitional residence for young adults. He has been taking courses in independent living skills, learning to shop for himself, doing laundry, and even working part time.

In 1988 Judi and Peter adopted Rehema, who was nine years old at the time and seventeen when I interviewed Judi. Born into a very poor family in Calcutta, she had gotten lost when she was about five and been taken to an orphanage where she was neglected. She has learning disabilities and attention-deficit disorder, and therefore needs special tutoring. But, says Judi, she is sociable, sweet, and talented at sewing.

Unexpectedly, Judi got pregnant and gave birth to a son, Jake, in 1989. But four siblings weren't enough. Rehema was desperate for a sister, Judi says, so she and Peter began the application process for another daughter. Then Peter changed his mind. This was a blow to Judi; it was rather like a miscarriage, she says. But after a workplace accident in which Peter almost died, he had a change of heart. They decided this time to adopt a girl from China. Peter had wanted a slightly older girl, but the daughter they adopted was thirteen months old. Never mind, it was love at first sight.

Adopting children with special needs requires a great deal of inner strength, and it imposes extra pressures on a couple. Judi knows of couples who have split up because the pressure was too great. Judi and Peter acknowledge this and on occasion give each other time off for separate vacations, and also work at finding time together, though this is rare. Judi has been active in their community, forming support groups, teaching about adoption, escorting children from India and China, and writing.

As Judi says, "There are no guarantees, in birth or in adoption. You just have to go with it."—and have an attitude that children are capable of doing a lot with disabilities if they are loved, nurtured, encouraged, and have parents who, like Judi and Peter, have faith in them. (See Appendix for more information on health issues.)

10

Answering Your Child's Questions About Being Adopted

In a postadoption workshop I attended, a woman recounted how her four-year-old daughter, having recently been told that she was adopted, bragged to all of her friends that she was a doctor. The conventional wisdom is to tell your child as early as possible about having been adopted, even if the concept is not immediately clear. Talking about it from the start introduces a comfort level with the idea, and will make it much easier for you to explain it to your child when the time comes to go into more detail. Certain aspects of adoption are very difficult for younger children to understand, particularly the concept of abandonment and, if this is your case, having no information about the birth parents. Your child may or may not want to know, but you should be prepared with answers in any case.

Basically, if you're at ease with your child's adoption, your child will be, too. The worst situation—and I've heard of numerous cases like this—is when the parents are so hung up about having adopted that they never tell their kids. Then when a medical crisis crops up and genetic information might be required, they suddenly have to tell.

So just make telling part of your lives!

Eileen and Jerry told their daughter and son, born to the same mother in Romania but to different fathers, that they were adopted almost as soon as they could communicate with them. Eileen routinely tells the cuddly and adorable Eli, who was not yet three when I first met him, "I'm so glad Elena had you in her tummy and gave birth to you so that I could hug you and take care of you forever."

Nanette and Rob freely discuss adoption all the time with their three-year-old Guatemalan-born daughter, Polly. "She calls herself 'Guatemollypolly'," says Nanette. There's no question that Polly was not born to Nanette and Rob; she looks very Indian. They take her to meetings of the Adoptive Parents Committee, where she is used to playing with children from all over the world. And at three, she is soon to have a sister who was born in Romania. Being part of a multicultural family has been made an open and welcome part of her upbringing.

Ava and Bob have often shown their son, Tim, photographs of the Russian orphanage where he had lived until they adopted him at age two, and have told him positive stories about his life there and of the care givers who helped raise him. When he was about four, he began asking about his birth mother. "He really wanted to know about her and felt sad about her," says Ava. It was more out of concern and curiosity, she thinks, than any longing to meet her, because he had been abandoned as an infant.

Miklos still writes to his care givers at the orphanage in Bulgaria where he lived for so long. Even though he has nearly lost all of his Bulgarian, his parents believe that Miklos needs to keep in touch with his birth country.

Keeping the cultural bonds alive can help, and you might want to remind your child that his or her biological mother most likely gave the child up in the hope that he or she would find a better home. And look where the child lives now and the type of family life he or she is enjoying!

Judi Kloper takes a proactive approach to raising her adopted children. She helped found a local adoption support group in her community and encourages community interest in Indian culture. But Judi knows of other families who have adopted children from other countries and are in apparent denial, doing nothing to promote their children's culture. Since the children are obviously not their biological offspring, Judi considers this a problem. "The kids need a positive self-image, and they're not getting it," she says.

Older children are more likely to retain memories of their early lives in their birth country. While we might think that life in a poor institution or foster home might be a negative experience, children may remember their playmates and some of the people who took care of them. It's often good to keep mementos of this time and to support your children's desire to hold on to pieces of their past, even if it's a blanket, a piece of clothing, or a fading photograph.

Treating Biological and Birth Children Equally

It's essential to treat adopted and biological children equally, and to incorporate their lives into the family with the same weight and energy. Jealousies can arise, as they did when Bethany and Karl's adopted daughter joined their two biological sons. But with the right preparation and sensitivity, a good balance can be found.

Bethany and Karl had one biological child, a son, when they first began thinking about adoption. "I'd heard about it on the radio and it just stuck," Barbara recalls. Living in a small resort town in the upper Midwest, Bethany and Karl did not have many direct adoption resources close at hand. But just as they began more serious research on adoption, Bethany became pregnant again and gave birth to their second son. Still, she remained interested in the idea and they began to explore it seriously.

They included their two sons in the process, and when they began preparing to adopt Adina from India, their sons wanted her crib to be in their room. "We read books to them and taught them about India," Bethany says. They also had a picture of Adina in the house; she was six months old at the time of her referral to them. When one of her older son's classmates asked who the person in the picture was, he said, "That's my sister." And when the friend then asked, "And how come she's dark?" he replied, "Oh, she was born in India." It was that easy. And he bonded quickly with Adina when she finally arrived.

The reality of having a baby sister was harder for Bethany and Karl's younger son. He wasn't the baby anymore. "He was hesitant, a bit difficult and jealous; he felt left out with all the attention I was giving to Adina. I had to say, 'I love you *exactly* the same as before.'"

The family also spent weeks of extra effort trying to make everyone feel comfortable. Adina, after all, had just been alone with Bethany for more than three weeks and was now competing with her new brothers for their mother's attention. She sometimes tried to push them away from Bethany and clung tight to her.

Furthermore, at eighteen months, Adina had already developed a personality of her own. Bethany quotes a friend who said that adopting a somewhat older child is a bit like marriage: in time you grow to understand the other person.

Now the family is completely bonded, and Bethany says she would love to consider another adoption from India.

Certainly, introducing any type of adoption into a family irrevocably alters how a family is formed. A family's cultural parameters change, too, especially when the child comes from a different racial background like Adina.

Judi Kloper says sometimes she feels that she almost has to

do extra for Jake, her biological son, just to remind him that he is *as* important as the other children!

In the very extended family of Sue and Hector Badeau (see Chapter 8), two of their twenty-one children are their biological offspring. They are treated no differently from the others and participate equally in the various cultural activities that the family undertakes. Sue and Hector's two internationally adopted children—Raj, born in India, and Jose, born in El Salvador—were given names reflective of their roots, but their culture has not been thrust on them. While Raj has pursued an interest in learning more about India, Jose has been much more passive about his birth country.

Finding Smart Answers to the Incredibly Naive Things People Say

As international adoption is becoming increasingly common, especially in university towns or large cities, it is not unusual to see more and more households that reflect this trend. No matter where you live, though, you can't escape from people who say naive, rude, or downright stupid things about your family.

There's one overall rule you should remember. When people ask you such questions in your child's presence, don't provide answers to please those people. Think foremost of your child's feelings. (See Appendix for the reference to Cheri Register's wonderful book *"Are Those Kids Yours?"*)

I asked all my interviewees to describe a few of the ignorant, unpleasant, and well-meaning-but-naive things people have said to them, and they shared some of their responses as well.

In Chapter 9, I described the challenges Judi Kloper has faced with several adopted children that have disabilities. Although she did not set out to adopt such children, over time Judi has learned that adopting special-needs children is a rewarding way to form a family. Once, when a neighbor saw her with Chandan, who is disabled with cerebral palsy, "he asked me if I was going to return him," says Judi. "I was just shocked. He's *my* child. How could anyone possibly say such a thing?" Such questions sometimes come as a surprise, and it's hard to know how to answer them. Usually, it pays not only to be polite, but also to try to educate, particularly other children, though many adults need it, too. And, if you can, in the right place and at the right time, come up with a snappy answer.

Answering the "Why Didn't You Adopt American?" Question

A frequently asked (and very annoying) question to families that do international adoption is "Why did you adopt overseas when there are so many American children who need homes?"

Alice, mother of Nadia, becomes very resentful at this question. But rather than explain how hard she did try at first to adopt an American child—only to be thwarted by the social services system in her state—she responds, "It's the decision that's best for *me.*"

Judi Kloper says that when people ask her that question, she retorts, "Why don't *you?*"

I had lived in South Africa for four years and began investigating adoption soon after I moved back to the United States. After considering a number of options, I focused on adopting from China. Some people asked why I didn't consider an African adoption or perhaps an African American adoption. I had inquired about adopting a black South African child when I lived there, but would not have been permitted to because I was a nonresident and over forty.

I also had to deal honestly and bluntly with my own personal limits. I didn't know if I could cope with an African American child. As a single mother, I wanted access to a support network. I didn't think adopting a black South African child alone would have been easy for me. And, like Alice, I wanted to make a decision that was best for *me* because that choice would ultimately be best for my child.

Patti and Peter, who adopted twin boys from Vietnam, are members of several support groups now: one for parents of children born in Vietnam, a parents-of-twins group in their neighborhood, and the local chapter of the Adoptive Parents Committee. People often do a double take when they see Patti, who is blond, strolling with her dark-haired Asian-looking sons. Initially, if Peter is not there, they assume that Patti's husband is Asian. But what makes Peter chuckle the most is when people ask, "Are they twins?" He likes the stock reply one couple in their twins group gives when the moment is right: "Twins! Oh, my god, they're really triplets. We must have lost one of them!"

Comments That Leave You Almost Speechless

• Some comments are so inappropriate that it is hard to know what to say. This is what Marion recalls after she brought her seven-year-old daughter to see a speech therapist. Her daughter is half Asian, half African American; Marion is Caucasian and also has a birth daughter. The therapist, doing an intake interview, asked Marion in front of her daughter, "Do you have any children of your own?"

The best response is "Yes, and you're looking at her."

• After Louise and Jack adopted seven-year-old Miklos from Bulgaria, Louise remembers only this surprisingly naive comment from a coworker: "Does your child call you Mom and Dad?"

• The husband of a friend who was in a supermarket with their Peruvian-born son sleeping in a Snugli was taken aback by this brusque question from a fellow shopper: "How much did you pay for *that* one?" He was too shaken up to think of an answer before the man had gone on to another aisle.

• When Judi gave birth to her son, Jake, after she and Peter had adopted three children, friends would ask, "Don't you love him more because he's your *real* child?" Judi recalls thinking, "I was almost worried that I wouldn't love him as *much*." Then, after she and her husband adopted a daughter from China, one person asked, "Will Dassi speak Chinese?"

• On the adoption bulletin boards, I have come across some stunningly cruel comments that parents have encountered and wanted to share with others. These included harshly anti-Asian criticisms that were uttered in front of the children. For example, a family was so taken aback by a racist comment made by an airline hostess that they wrote down the hostess's name, contacted the airline, and received a letter saying that she had been disciplined. You *don't* need to take these comments quietly!

• I have encountered quite a few well-meaning comments about my daughter-to-be that I just laughed off. "She'll probably be great in math and science," said a relative. "Chinese children are *so* well behaved, you'll have no problem," mentioned a friend. A child, seeing a photograph of my daughter, mimicked his image of an Asian person. His embarrassed mother tried to dismiss it. The best policy, when the person is not there, is to let some of these comments go. Your adopted child will most likely pick up many of your own personality traits, strengths, and weaknesses—and will have many of his or her own as well. And that is how it should be. They are individuals.

Using Positive Adoption Language

It's important to be sensitive in the way you use language to discuss adoptions. I make mistakes myself a lot, still, when I'm not really thinking. But I'm getting better at it! Nanette is blunt about correcting me. "It's not 'she had children of her own' and also adopted," she once scolded me, when I said that about a woman I know. "They're *all* her own. It's just that some were birth children and others were adopted."

Nanette caught me another time, when I referred to a "foreign adoption." "It's *international* or *intercountry* adoption," she said, correcting me. I don't make the mistake anymore.

"My Out-of-Body Experience"

My friend Nicole had the best response of all when friends and strangers alike asked whether she regretted not having a biological child. Her daughter, Chiara, who was born in China, is as precious and close to her as any child she would rear. "She *is* my biological child," she sometimes says to them, as they look on curiously with raised eyebrows. "She's my 'out-of-body experience'!"

Adoption newsletters and magazines often have lists of positive and negative terms. Here's one list to bear in mind. It's worth learning to say it right.[1]

Positive Language	Negative Language
Birth parent	Real parent
Biological parent	Natural parent
Birth child	Own child
My child	Adopted child
Born to single parents	Illegitimate
Terminated parental rights	Give up
Make an adoption plan	Give away
To parent	To keep
Waiting child	Adoptable child; available child
Making contact with	Reuniting
Parent	Adoptive parent
International adoption	Foreign adoption

[1] From *Adoptalk* newsletter, February 1995. *Adoptalk* is published by New York State Adoptive Parents Committee, Inc. For information, write to APC, P.O. Box 3525, Church Street Station, New York, New York 10008-3525.

Positive Language	Negative Language
Adoption triad	Adoption triangle
Permission to sign a release	Disclosure
Search	Track down parents
Child placed for adoption	An unwanted child
Court termination	Child taken away
Child with special needs	Handicapped child
Child from abroad	Foreign child
Was adopted	Is adopted

A Short Final Note

Adoption is wonderful! Enjoy the gift that it is. I hope this book will help you make wise choices that enable you to build a loving family. Please let me know how this book has helped, and let me know if you have encountered other experiences or resources that would be valuable for future publication. You can write me care of my publisher.

Appendix

Organizations, Publications, and Other Resources

ORGANIZATIONS

International Concerns for Children (ICC)

911 Cypress Drive
Boulder, Colorado 80303
Fax and phone: (303)494-8333

If you're looking for broad information on adoption or haven't decided where to start, ICC should be your *first stop*. This voluntary organization does a phenomenal job of compiling the most current information available on issues relating to adoption, on the countries where adoption takes place, and on agencies in each state and the countries where they have programs. ICC's monthly updates of agency information, a key source for adoption professionals, is critical, since agency programs and costs often change as do country programs themselves because of new laws and problems that may arise.

ICC provides the following:

1. The annual *Report on Intercountry Adoption,* plus ten monthly updates. This *essential* book includes approximate costs, waiting peri-

ods, and the types of children available from dozens of agencies and other organizations that ICC deems, according to its brochure, to be working "in morally, ethically, and legally correct ways for adoptive placement in North American homes." The book lists requirements for parents, including single parent families, describes the I-600 orphan visa procedure, discusses medical issues, and has an array of articles that provide guidance in understanding the needs of adopted children. ($25 donation)

The listings of agencies also include their program fees, but the fees are not costed out, so if a particular program intrigues you, ask the agency exactly what their fees cover and what they don't. One well-known New York City–based agency offers sliding scales for its services, but the intercountry report only lists its lowest fee rather than the fee range. I feel that this is misleading. No one I know who has used this agency has paid the lowest fee for an intercountry adoption, and a single friend with no extra income who considered using its services found that no discount would be available to her. One couple who has used this agency twice paid approximately $20,000 for each of their two adoptions from Ecuador.

2. A one-year subscription with monthly updates to an adoption photo listing of children in their birth countries for whom agencies are seeking placements. These are mostly older than young school-age children, and some have siblings who must be placed together. Also, some have medical conditions that can either be easily corrected or are very minor uncorrectable conditions. ($20 donation)

3. A quarterly newsletter with information on refugees, sponsorships, legislation, medical issues and health care, and adoption ($10 donation). It also includes useful press clippings of recent coverage on adoption issues.

4. Papers and brochures to assist adoptive families ($2.50–$3 each). One paper written by an adult Korean adoptee contained much information that I found very useful in preparing me for my adoption from China.

5. Counseling service on adoption provided by experienced adoptive families. A number of the people I interviewed for the book of-

fered emphatic praise of the work done by ICC. It is an excellent starting point to learn more about the issues surrounding international adoption, including what types of children are waiting for homes, specific country issues, and critical medical and health concerns.

Adoptive Families of America (AFA)

3333 Highway 100 North
Minneapolis, MN 55422
(800)372-3300; http://www.adoptfam.com

AFA is a nonprofit membership organization that campaigns on behalf of adoptions of all types. It is the publisher of *Adoptive Families* magazine. It is an important unified voice that advocates in favor of legislation to help adoptive families get tax relief for adoption expenses and obtain recognition of adoption as a way of forming families.

It also offers a catalog service to order books, audiotapes, videotapes, and other products related to adoption, such as multicultural toys and greeting cards.

National Adoption Center (NAC)

1500 Walnut Street, Suite 701
Philadelphia, PA 19102
(215)735-9988 or (800)TO-ADOPT; fax: (215)735-9410
http://www.adopt.org/adopt

NAC focuses on campaigning to find families for U.S. waiting children, but its advocacy of employer support for adoption is important for parents pursuing international adoption. At the time this book went to press, Suzanne Kemp at NAC was completing a three-year study funded by the Kellogg Foundation to survey which businesses already provide support and what the nature of that support is, as well as to campaign for more businesses to do so. It lists several hundred corporations and universities that offer financial assistance, paid leave, flextime, counseling, and other services for employees seeking to adopt children.

NAC publishes the excellent brochure *Looking At the Business Case: Why Adoption Benefits?* It includes a sample of an adoption assistance reimbursement form and examines why adoptions are so expensive and how businesses benefit by providing support to their employees who adopt children.

National Adoption Information Clearinghouse (NAIC)

5640 Nicholson Lane, Suite 300
Rockville, MD 20852
(301)231-6512; fax: (301)984-8527

NAIC operates under contract to the Administration on Children and Families of the U.S. Department of Health and Human Services and provides a wide range of resource material to prospective adoptive parents. While much of it focuses on domestic issues, NAIC's list of brochures, books, and other resources (including adoption support groups) can provide information for any type of adoptive situation. Some materials are free of charge while others require a minimal payment.

NAIC's products and services include:

• brochures on many aspects of adoption, most for $2.50–$3 each, including one on intercountry adoption
• books, catalogs, and directories that run from $15 to $25, including a national adoption directory and a publications and services catalog
• current information on adoption-related legislation (the materials are of principal interest to lawyers doing adoption and can be hefty and expensive to reproduce)
• referrals of adoption agencies
• adoption support groups by state
• names of experts in specific fields
• a computerized bibliography on adoption, by topic

National Council for Single Adoptive Parents, Inc. (NCSAP)

> P.O. Box 15084
> Chevy Chase, MD 20825
> (202)966-6367

NCSAP's founder, Hope Marindin, wrote and published *The Handbook for Single Adoptive Parents* listed below. NCSAP publishes a quarterly newsletter for $18 a year.

Parent Network for Post-Institutionalized Children (for parents of children with attachment disorders)

> P.O. Box 613
> Meadowlands, PA 15347
> (412)222-6009

Center Kids (for gay and lesbian parents and all types of parenting) The Family Project of the Lesbian and Gay Community Services Center of New York

> Community Services Center of New York
> 208 West 13th Street
> New York, New York 10011
> (212)620-7310

Children of Lesbians and Gays Everywhere (COLAGE) (for gay and lesbian parents and all types of parenting)

> 2300 Market Street, #165
> San Francisco, CA 94114
> (415)583-8029

PUBLICATIONS

Books for Parents

Family Bonds: Adoption and the Politics of Parenting by Elizabeth Bartholet (Boston: Houghton Mifflin Company, 1993). Bartholet, a Harvard law professor and adoptive mother of two boys from Peru (and birth mother of one son), touches on some of the thorny social issues that still make the choice to adopt seem like a stigma or the second-best (or desperate) choice of parents seeking to form a family if they are unable to do so, or choose not to, through biological means. I wasn't ready to read her book until my own adoption was well under way. Then I often found myself nodding at the rightness of some of her comments. But I'm happy to report that many of the emotional, social, and logistical obstacles that used to impede international adoption—particularly by single men and women and so-called older parents over forty—have pretty much gone by the wayside. I am about ten years younger than Bartholet and did my adoption a decade years later, and found that people like her had done a wonderful and important job in paving the way for me and many friends who adopted when they were in their forties. (I was, however, astonished to read her quote of $3,000 to $4,000 for a home study.) If you're looking for an empathetic first-person account of the challenges and gratification of adoption, Bartholet is on the mark.

International Adoption: Sensitive Advice for Prospective Parents, by Jean Knoll and Mary-Kate Murphy (Chicago Review Press, 1994). I gave this book to Irene, a single mother whose experiences I have cited in my book, before she left for her first trip to Paraguay to meet her daughter and undergo some of the stressful legal and other procedures (including a psychological examination) necessary to complete her adoption. The book primarily contains the personal accounts of international adoptions that the authors undertook, one from Korea, the other from Peru, with anecdotes of other adoptive parents interspersed. Irene said that the book helped sustain her through the immense emotional pressures she was feeling, especially after her departure had been delayed several times and her papers had been lost twice in Paraguay by the translator (and were found each time several days later, while she sweated blood in the interim), and she feared that still more could go wrong. Also, she was essentially alone. I was particularly moved by the postscript, "Tell me the story again, Mama," in which coauthor Jean Knoll describes a fantasy version of how her own daughter's birth mother gave her up and how she came to find her. This book is great for moral support and affirmation.

"Are Those Kids Yours?": American Families with Children Adopted from Other Countries by Cheri Register (New York: The Free Press,

1991). Many adoptive parents refer to Register's book as the principal resource to guide them through the sometimes troublesome encounters with people who ask naive though usually well-meaning questions about our having children who do not look like us. (Some of the questions, however, are downright nasty.) Her main point is that you shouldn't avoid the questions: your children will pick up on your avoidance. And you shouldn't put the onus on your child to answer, either. Approaches can vary from direct answers to humor.

One parent in the book is quoted as saying, "The most compelling reason for tact is not to kill rudeness with kindness, but to spare our children from hurt. I tried, for a while to mask my irritation with the added force of pride: 'Yes, these are my two beautiful daughters and I'm so glad they are.' I hoped it would put my children at ease, but instead it made me uncomfortable. My answer objectified them just as much as the question did. So then I tried passing some of the questions on to Grace, who was four at the time, to demonstrate that she could indeed hear and understand English. When I heard her answer a simple 'Hi, how are you?' with 'I was born in Korea and so was my sister,' I decided it was not fair to put her on the spot. From then on I have given short, unembellished, and sometimes misleading answers— 'How long have you had them?' 'Oh, forever.'—and then averted my eyes to discourage any more questions. Once Grace asked, in a stage whisper, 'Do you like that?' That was the cue that I needed to explain my feelings and check on hers. Now we make jokes like 'Wher'dja git those kids? At K-Mart?' and Maria pinches the dog's face and says, 'Ooooh, you got such chubby cheeks.' "

Making Sense of Adoption: A Parents' Guide by Lois Ruskai Melina (New York: Perennial Library/Solstice Press, 1989). Melina, also the author of *Raising Adopted Children*, has put together a user-friendly book that addresses the types of questions and issues you may confront as you undertake your adoption, prepare for your child, and then raise your child. Although intercountry adoption forms just a part of the book, many of the activities Melina recommends are useful no matter what type of adoption was involved. It has an excellent annotated listing of ninety books for children on adoption (and how to get them if they're not easily available in local bookstores) and a good bibliography for adults. Melina is also the editor of the newsletter *Adopted Child.*

The Whole Life Adoption Book: Realistic Advice for Building a Healthy Adoptive Family by Jayne E. Schooler (Colorado Springs, Colorado: Pinon Books, 1993). I like the structure of this book, which deals with all types of adoptions and the dilemmas adoptive families face. Its four sections cover the choice to adopt ("Choosing to Love a Stranger" is the provocative title of the first chapter); adjusting to the child's arrival at home; communicating about adoption both among parents and with children; and creating a nurturing family, with special attention to the needs of adopted adolescents and to transcultural adoptions. It contains many good case studies, and also examines the different approaches that people may take, including those who choose to delay discussing adoption and those who advocate doing it much earlier (the author prefers the latter).

Talking with Young Children About Adoption by Mary Watkins and Susan Fisher (New Haven: Yale University Press, 1993). This book includes case studies and works through sample questions that children ask at different stages of their lives and how to answer them. A number of the case studies consider international adoptions, although neither the table of contents nor the index help you know which ones. I found some of the stories quite interesting—I read the book before I had adopted—especially one about a little girl born in India whose adoptive mother (also single) worries about how to discuss birthmother issues with her daughter, and comes to realize that although her daughter already understands the difference between a birth mother and her adoptive mother, she does not seem to be "all consumed" by learning more about her roots. Some children are just that way, the mother realizes, but she is glad she has coped with it when her child was very young. As a postscript, the book also examines two case studies in which adoption was either discussed in a very low-key way in a family or delayed until the two children (both adopted as newborns) are much older, in this case eight and nine. The authors obviously prefer much earlier disclosure and discuss what children can actually conceptualize at the difference stages of growing up.

Adopt International by O. Robin Sweet and Patty Bryan (New York: Noonday Books, 1996). This book gives an overview on the basic steps necessary to accomplish an international adoption and provides state-by-state listings of agencies, support organizations, newsletters,

INS offices, social services departments, and other resources to help the adoption process.

Real Parents, Real Children: Parenting the Adopted Child by Holly van Gulden and Lisa Bartels-Robb (New York: Crossroads Publishing Company, 1993). This exceptionally thorough book, written by two of the preeminent adoption experts in the United States, advises parents when and how to discuss adoption at different stages in their children's lives, from early childhood to young adulthood. It not only provides many activities to guide families through stages of the life cycle, but is full of resources for further reading. International adoption gets significant mention.

Transracial Adoption: Children and Parents Speak by Constance Pohl and Kathy Harris (New York: Franklin Watts, 1992). This book delves into many of the very sensitive—and sometimes politicized—issues associated with transracial adoptions, especially those involving white families adopting African American children. It also has sections on Korean and Latin American adoptions and the racial and cultural issues these often involve. (The book was published when Chinese adoptions were still very new.)

The Adoption Reader: Birth Mothers, Adoptive Mothers and Adopted Daughters Tell Their Stories, edited by Susan Wadia-Ells (Seattle, Washington: Seal Press, 1995). Many of the stories that are told here pertain to the emotional experiences of domestic adoptions, including those of women who gave up babies for adoption and the reunions (or attempted ones) with birth mothers; just a few focus on international adoptions. Yet the writing here is so good, and the experiences being described transcend the types of adoptions being written about. Hearing from a middle-class U.S.-born woman on the loss she still feels decades later on giving up her first birth child could perhaps be the story of a woman in Ecuador, China, India, or Romania who also had to give up her birth child. Carol Austin's contribution, "Latent Tendencies and Covert Acts," describes how, as politically active lesbians, she and her partner had to go back into the closet in order to adopt a child from Peru. In their case, her partner was the one who did the adoption, attending meetings, getting information, and doing the paperwork, although she joined her partner in actually going to Peru to navigate through the courts and to complete the adoption. Editor Susan Wadia-Ells chronicles her trip to India to adopt her son, Anil, and Denise Sherer Jacobson describes how she and her husband, who both have cerebral palsy, decided to adopt a child and then had to plot out the logistics on how they would do it in a world that did not believe that they could.

Books for Single Adoptive Parents

The Handbook for Single Adoptive Parents, compiled and edited by Hope Marindin (Committee for Single Adoptive Parents, Chevy Chase, MD 20825, updated edition, 1992).

Those among us who are single and have adopted children have to pay special attention to financial, guardianship, and medical issues, among other things, when there is no partner to assume responsibility in case of an emergency. This book includes a medical primer by Dr. Jerri Ann Jenista, one of the preeminent specialists in this field (see also Chapter 5 and Appendix). You will find many valuable pointers on coping through first-person accounts by other single parents. As we venture into adoption, many of us learn almost by osmosis about the need to create a support system for ourselves.

The Single Parent Family: Living Happily in a Changing World by Marge Kennedy and Janet Spencer King (New York: Crown Publishers, 1994). This is a great book for nuts-and-bolts advice on handling a family as a single parent. (Single dads get their share of time, by the way.) Although it *does not* specifically address adoption issues, it does cover many of the challenges that you are likely to confront as a single parent. Advice covers family-time management, financial planning, dating, and each chapter offers a Q&A by professionals in the field. There's particular emphasis on making sure the parent meets her and his needs, too. You must, for example, make sure you give yourself time to do *your* things.

Single Mothers by Choice: A Guidebook for Single Women Who Are Considering or Have Chosen Motherhood by Jane Mattes, CSW (New York: Times Books, 1994). Jane Mattes is the founder of Single Mothers by Choice, and this book addresses a range of questions for single mothers who give birth and who adopt. One of her important points is that your son or daughter will likely benefit from having someone willing to play a fatherlike role. In one case study, she describes how a single mother approached a man she knew who was happily married—and happily childless—but was willing to develop an ongoing fatherlike relationship with her son. Of course, it was necessary to clarify that he had a separate life with his own wife and would not be available all the time. But he would be there, and in times of crisis, the child should certainly feel welcome to call.

Books for Children

A Mother for Choco by Keiko Kasza (New York: PaperStar/PaperStar, Putnam & Grosset Group, 1996). First published in Japan in 1982, *A Mother for Choco* is now an adoption classic. It tells in the simplest language the touching tale of a little bird who has lost its parents and is finally taken in by a loving mother bear—who, coincidentally, also plays mother to an orphaned piglet, baby alligator, and young hippopotamus. It's a sweet book and is an easy introduction to the idea that children and parents don't have to look alike to be a family.

Horace by Holly Keller (New York: Greenwillow Books, 1991). Written on a more advanced level than *A Mother for Choco*, *Horace* is the story of a spotted cat who is being raised by striped cats. Whenever his mother tries to tell him the story of his birth, he falls asleep. But one day, Horace wanders off in search of his real parents and discovers a family of spotted cats like himself. They invite him to join them, and he plays with them gleefully, but at the end of the day, he realizes he misses his parents and returns home. Like *A Mother for Choco*, *Horace* deals directly with the identity crises young children in transcultural families sometimes face. The story is delicate and moving.

A Forever Family: A Child's Story About Adoption, stories and pictures by Roslyn Banish, with Jennifer Jordan-Wong (New York: HarperTrophy, 1992). Written with five- to eight-year-olds in mind, this book tells in simple language the autobiography of Jennifer, who was placed in her first foster home at age three, her second at age six, and finally adopted at age seven. Her adoptive father is Chinese

American, so Jennifer has Chinese-born grandparents on one side. (Her other set of grandparents died before she was born.) I found myself becoming teary-eyed at her simple story. A sweet girl, she knows that she is loved, but she also comes across as lonely and puzzled at her plight. One of her foster families was a black family; it is unclear from the story or her photograph if Jennifer is white or perhaps has a mixed background. She remains close to her foster parents and, as she grows up in a nurturing environment, may come to appreciate the richness of the unusual childhood that she has had. The book suggests that this is possible, and although Jennifer remains unresolved about her biological mother, she recognizes that she is now someplace permanent.

We Adopted You, Benjamin Koo by Linda Walvoord Girard, illustrated by Linda Shute (Morton Grove, IL: Albert Whitman & Co., 1989). Written as a first-person account by a teenager, but targeting younger readers, this sweet book tells how Benjamin was adopted, how he reacted to his new family (and they to him), and many of the experiences he has in school and his neighborhood. It also looks at what happens when his parents adopt a daughter—his sister—who was born in Brazil. It gently addresses the cultural dilemmas Benjamin and his sister encounter and the way they and their parents learn to respond. This is actually a great book for adults, too. It doesn't sugarcoat the problems; it does address some of the pains that adopted children may feel. And it is very affirming and joyful.

Families Are Different, written and illustrated by Nina Pellegrini (New York: Holiday House, 1991). An easy reader told in the first person by a young adopted Korean girl, this book shows that families can be diverse: interracial, large, single parent, etc.

How It Feels to Be Adopted by Jill Krementz (New York: Alfred A. Knopf, 1982). For many of the nineteen young people aged eight through sixteen (most in the older group) who were interviewed for this book, this was the first time they had been asked to discuss what it meant to be adopted. In short profiles, which include photographs by the author of the youngsters alone and with their families, they describe the occasional dilemmas they face about being adopted; or, as one boy writes, the "embarrassment" of being adopted: "There's another kid I know who's adopted, and he's always getting into trouble. It really makes me upset when people say to me, 'Oh, you're adopted just like him—you two should stick together!' He's a kid who talks back to teachers and writes on the wall—stuff like that. I don't even want to be near him."

Happy Adoption Day by John McCutcheon (Boston: Little, Brown & Co., 1996). Written as a simple song—the musical accompaniment is in the back—this book celebrates the day that a child was adopted into his or her family, and applies to any type of adoption. It's very colorful and very easy.

Let's Talk About Adoption by Fred Rogers (New York: G.P. Putnam's Sons, 1994). This feel-good book, by the children's television star Mr. Rogers, examines the ways that families are formed through adoption and emphasizes the ideas of sharing and belonging. It uses very simple language and excellent photos to focus on three different types of adoptive families.

When You Were Born in China by Sara Dorow and *When You Were Born in Korea* by Brian Boyd (St. Paul, MN: Yeong and Yeong Book Company, 1996 and 1993, respectively). *When You Were Born in China* is the first book to examine explicitly the experience of a child adopted from China. Using text (at a fourth-grade reading level; best if parents read it to their children) and many photographs, it introduces much of the experience of parents traveling to China to get their daughters (and in rare cases, sons) and what their family lives have been like. It grapples with sensitivity the reason girls are abandoned. The second book uses a similar format, although the experience of Korean adoptions is different because the children are usually brought to the United States with an escort. Note: These two books can be obtained by contacting Adoptive Families of America (see information at the beginning of this section).

For Children and Adults

Growing Up Adopted by Maxine Rosenberg (New York: Bradbury Press, 1989). Written for teenagers and adults, this book provides first-person accounts by adoptees ranging in age from eight to forty-eight.

This is just the type of book I'd been looking for, since one of my greatest anxieties was about how I could be an effective single parent and prepare to raise my child to appreciate my culture and her culture—well, actually, *our* culture. This book may help answer questions you also have. It has a useful list of resources.

To me one of the most affecting anecdotes was by Marsha, who was forty-two when she told her story. She remembers learning at age seven—much too late—that she had been adopted. This revelation came only after she had heard in school about how babies were born and she went back to confirm it with her mother. No, her mother had to admit, Marsha didn't develop in *her* womb, and then she explained precisely what had happened. "Nothing could have stunned me more." Marsha recalls. "Until then I had felt totally a part of my family and especially loved by my grandmother. Suddenly everything seemed different." The lesson here, says Marsha, is that parents should be open and comfortable about discussing adoption as early as possible, even if a child doesn't fully comprehend what it means.

Magazines

Adoptive Families
   3333 Highway 100 North
   Minneapolis, MN 55422
   (612)535-4829; fax: (612)535-7808
   This is my personal favorite. The magazine does a wonderful job covering just about everything and keeping it up to date. There's also a section for pen pals for your children. Each issue includes articles on the milestones and problems adopted children sometimes confront as they grow up. Plus, you can learn about companies that offer products such as books, toys, music, and greeting cards made especially for adoptive families.

Roots and Wings
   P.O. Box 638
   Chester, NJ 07930
   (908)637-8828; Web page: http://www.adopting.org/rw.html
   (also Rootswing@aol.com)
   This is a newer magazine that you also may enjoy and offers comprehensive coverage on international adoption.

F.A.C.E. Facts
Families Adopting Children Everywhere
P.O. Box 28058
Northwood Station
Baltimore, MD 21239
(410)488-2656

Gay and Lesbian Adoption Reading Packet (1996 update)
c/o Wayne Steinman
1171 Capodanno Boulevard
Staten Island, NY 10306
E-mail: CenterKids@aol.com; GLPCI@aol.com
A gay father of an adopted child, Steinman has compiled an enormous collection of articles and pamphlets under one cover that examine the dynamics, legal concerns, and costs, as well as other resources (agencies, support organizations, a bibliography) of particular interest to gay and lesbian parents. It covers all types of adoptions.

Newsletters

Adopted Child
P.O. Box 9362
Moscow, ID 83843
(208)882-1794
This newsletter is edited by Lois Ruskai Melina, author of *Raising Adopted Children* and *Making Sense of Adoption* (see above).

Single Parents with Adopted Kids
4108 Washington Road, #101
Kenosha, WI 53144

The POST
Box 613
Meadowlands, PA 15347
(412)222-6009
Produced by the Parent Network for Post-Institutionalized Children, this quarterly newsletter covers all facets of attachment disorder and provides resource information on where and how to get treatment and new research developments in the field. Started by four parents as a voluntary initiative, the newsletter costs just $15 a year. The Parent

Network also organizes conferences and has videotapes and related products for sale.

Newsletters That Focus on International Adoption

The African Connection
Americans for African Adoptions Inc. (AAFA)
8910 Timberwood Drive
Indianapolis, IN 46234
(317)271-4567; fax: (317)271-8739
AAFA is one of two agencies that does placements from Africa, and works mainly in Ethiopia, Mali, Rwanda, and Sierra Leone; Family Connections (in Modesto, California) works in Ethiopia. Many of the available children are older and have come from extremely impoverished backgrounds and experience a substantial culture shock in the United States. It's an interesting opportunity for families up to a genuine challenge. The costs for these adoptions are much lower than for most other international adoptions, and siblings are often available. The children are escorted to the United States.

Buenas Noticias
Latin American Parents Association—National Capital Region
P.O. Box 4403
Silver Spring, MD 20914-4403
(301)431-3407

China Connection
Christian World Adoption
6620 Shingle Ridge Road S.W.
Roanoke, VA 24018

Connections (focus on children from the Indian subcontinent)
1417 East Miner
Arlington Heights, IL 60004

Copihue
USCAF (United States Chilean Adoptive Families)
2041 North 107th Street
Milwaukee, WI 53227
(414)257-0248

Filipinas
  Filipinas Publishing
  655 Sutter, #333
  San Francisco, CA 94102
  (800)654-7777

Limiar: USA (Brazilian focus)
  11 Atterbury Boulevard, #4
  Hudson, OH 44236
  (216)653-8129

Open Arms (Indian focus)
  6816 135th Court N.E.
  Redmond, WA 98052
  (206)869-0444

Que Tal
  Latin American Parents Association (LAPA)
  P.O. Box 339
  Brooklyn, NY 11234
  (718)236-8689

Spice Rack (Indian focus)
  c/o Lynn Beard McMillan
  604 Rollingwood Drive
  Greensboro, NC 27410
  Also sponsors four-day summer Indian culture camp program.

PRODUCTS FOR ADOPTIVE FAMILIES

Adoption Option Cards & Gifts

  P.O. Box 6883
  Tacoma, WA 98407
  (206)759-7089

Send for free brochure for "renewable" adoption book and other products.

Adoptive Families of America (AFA) Bookstore

> 3333 Highway 100 North
> Minneapolis, MN 55422
> (612)535-4829; fax: (612)535-7808

Adoptive Families devotes at least two pages in each issue to books for adults and children, multicultural toys, and other materials on adoption. Recent offerings included Chinese Barbie and Kenya Barbie, and videos for children on adoption.

Tapestry Books

> P.O. Box 359, Dept. C-4
> Ringoes, NJ 08551
> (800)765-2367

Ask for a free catalog.

ON-LINE RESOURCES (See also Chapter 2, "The Technology Revolution")

Several on-line services have adoption information. My experience has been with America Online, which, at this writing, appears to have the most comprehensive offerings, with adoption "chats" and many bulletin boards covering more than two dozen topics (and the number seems to expand all the time). This serves as an excellent and up-to-date information resource. (CompuServe and Prodigy also have adoption resources, but I have not explored them.)

You can download much of the material and then either read it in a word-processing program or print it out so that you do not have to spend as much time (and money) on-line. I found on-line resources particularly useful in locating interviewees for this book around the country who were involved in a range of different types of adoptions. I also had the pleasure of meeting a number of people in person as a result. Later, as my own adoption progressed, especially from the date of my referral to the time I finally came home, I went on-line regularly to ask questions and share experiences.

The investment in on-line resources can save you money and time. I have learned of many services to facilitate adoption and get information, such as obtaining faxed materials from INS on U.S. government policies on adoption and special issues relating to China (see Chapter 2). In addition, a growing number of adoption agencies now have Web pages that describe their programs and often their fees. On-line services are creating new markets *and* competition among agencies, which ultimately is good for you: you can get much more information, and as the agencies compete for clients, they will also have to offer improved services and programs.

To find out what is available, you need to access your on-line service and then type in the keyword "Adoption." Then click on the subjects you are interested in. On-line adoption chats and bulletin boards give you the opportunity to seek referrals on agencies you might be thinking of using or recommendations of agencies that you may not know about that have a good record of placing children from the country you might be interested in adopting from. You can find out about the good and bad experiences people have had, and obtain the most up-to-date information on which agencies have good programs and which are having problems. Note: The bulletin boards are monitored by adoption experts to prevent their abuse by individuals seeking to solicit clients. You will rarely see agencies advertising on the bulletin boards.

The on-line services include:

• Adoption chats several times a week
• Adoption libraries of information on almost every issue related to foreign adoption. I was able to do country-specific research on issues related to adopting from Russia, Vietnam, the Philippines, India, Brazil, Korea, Latin America, China, and Eastern Europe. The topics keep growing as more participants join the discussions and seek new information. On China alone, because so many adoptions are taking place there, three separate discussion groups were on-line, one on the ABC's of adopting in China, another on travel to China, and the third on raising children born in China.
• Files of past adoption chats that you can download and print out. I have found some of these invaluable in reading about other

peoples' experiences locating good agencies (and winnowing out those that are not so good); tracking changes in different countries that affected adoptions; and learning about some of the specific issues and problems waiting parents or adoptive parents confront once their children are home.

The World Wide Web is a growing source of information. More and more agencies have Web pages that will provide you information on their services and some of their specific country programs. Some agencies will also provide you with photo listings, although you will need a fast modem (at least 14.4 kps) to gain access to the graphics. Use a Web browser (such as Webcrawler) to get a listing of agencies and you will discover a wealth of Web pages for different organizations and publications. (My Web browser indicated that there were 16,000 topics under "adoption agencies," though a few referred to animal adoption and others were off on a totally different track!) Here's just a sampling of Internet addresses (they'll provide addresses for country-specific programs):

- Adoption Research Newsletter: http://www.fsci.umn.edu/cyfc/AdoptInfo/ARN.htm (tends to be academic-oriented)
- AdoptioNetwork: http://www.adoption.org/adopt
- Adoptive Families of America: http://www.adoptivefam.org
- Families with Children from China: http://www.catalog.com/fwcfc/
- Latin American Adoptive Families: http://www.gems.com/adoption/laaf
- Rainbow Kids (an on-line resource on international adoption): http://www.rainbowkids.com
- *RootsWings* magazine: http://www.adopting.org/rw.html (also: Rootswing@aol.com)
- Russian adoption mailing list: http://www.serve.com/~fredt/adopt.html
- Russian adoption network: http://www.moscow.com/resources/adoption/adoption.html
- Tapestry Books (specializing in adoption): http://www.webcom.com/~tapestry/

EMPLOYER SUPPORT FOR ADOPTION

Enlightened companies are increasingly adding adoption support to their family benefits packages. This support recognizes that adoptive families do have special needs as well as share many of the same needs as new birth parents.
Two good sources for information are:

1. "100 Best Companies for Working Mothers" by Milt Moskowitz and Carol Townsend *(Working Mother,* October 1995), which lists the benefits packages of companies that accommodate family needs, including adoption support, beyond the twelve weeks unpaid leave time and guaranteed job security required by the Family Leave Medical Act (FMLA). Many of these companies also offer flextime, compressed workweeks, part-time and job-sharing possibilities and work-at-home. Among the top one hundred, eighty-five have some sort of adoption support.

Best adoption financial aid, according to *Working Mother*
Up to $6,000: Fannie Mae
Up to $5,000: Blue Cross and Blue Shield of Massachusetts, Calvert Group, Du Pont Merck, Fel-Pro, Hallmark Cards, Hewitt Associates, HBO, KPMG Peat Marwick, MBNA America Bank
Up to $4,000: Dow Chemical, Quad/Graphics
Up to $3,000: Amgen, CMP Publications, Johnson & Johnson, Lancaster Labs, Leo Burnett, Mattel, Mentor Graphics, NYNEX, Riverside Methodist Hospitals, SAS Institute, Xerox

2. The National Adoption Center survey mentions many of the companies recognized by *Working Mother* as well as universities and state governments that have adoption-related benefits. The following employers not in *Working Mother* offer reimbursement of at least

$4,000: Borden, Builder's Square, Chubb Group, Dispatch Printing Co., Donnelly Corp., FMC Corp, Hasbro, Household International, Johns Hopkins University, Little Caesars, Microsoft, Millipore, Monsanto, Motorola, Owens-Corning, Silicon Graphics, The Stanley Works, State of South Carolina, University of South Carolina, and Wendy's International.

HEALTH INFORMATION RELATED TO ADOPTION

Physical health information on adopted children

• The International Adoption Clinic was established by Dr. Dana Johnson, who is also on the board of Adoptive Families of America and is an adoptive father.

The clinic will provide you with a checklist of articles and information specifically tied to adoption health issues. Some are country-specific (relating to children adopted from Romania, Korea, China, India, or the Philippines), and some look at specific health concerns (hepatitis B, cytomegalovirus, tuberculosis). Others are of more general interest, including a booklet on the medical evaluation of internationally adopted children and screening tests used for international adoptees. These booklets will help you recognize if your child is reaching developmental milestones appropriate for children adopted from other countries.

To get the checklist, contact

International Adoption Clinic
Box 211, UMHC
420 Delaware Street, SE
Minneapolis, MN 55455
(612)626-2928; Fax: (612)624-8176

• Dr. Jerri Ann Jenista is one of the most prolific authors on health issues connected to adoption. She is the editor of *Adoption/Medical News*, a newsletter published ten times a year, which provides updated information on specific medical and developmental issues pertaining to adoption. For subscription information, contact

Adoption Advocates Press
   1921 Ohio Street, NE
   Palm Bay, FL 32907
   Fax: (407)724-0815

You can also contact Dr. Jenista directly at the

Department of Pediatrics
F7828/0244, C.S. Mott Children's Hospital
University of Michigan Medical Center
1500 East Medical Center Drive
Ann Arbor, MI 48109-0244

• *Health Information for International Travel* is a publication highly recommended by Dr. Jenista and is issued annually by the Department of Health and Human Services to provide specific information on immunization requirements and foreign health risks. Information is listed by country and by diseases; references for emergency health care when you are overseas are also listed. It costs just $4.75, and here's where to get it:

HHS Publication No. (CDC) 85-8280
Superintendent of Documents
U.S. Government Printing Office
Washington, DC 20402
(202)783-3238

You can also get information on specific foreign health issues by calling regional U.S. Public Health Services quarantine stations. They can be contacted as follows:

Chicago: (312)686-2150
Honolulu: (808)541-2552
Los Angeles: (213)215-2365
Miami: (305)526-2910

Index

About the Author

Myra Alperson began writing this book around the time she submitted her application to an adoption agency for an infant girl from China. As she describes here, it was not a straightforward process; there were several logistical delays, and she paused a few times herself as she questioned whether or not she really had the courage to go through with the adoption.

In July 1996 the decision to adopt became irrevocable when she received a phone call from her agency informing her that a referral had come through for a six-and-a-half-month-old infant girl. A photograph of the child with her medical history, along with travel advice and other information, were sent the next day.

When Myra opened the envelope the following morning and saw the tiny color photograph of the beautiful child who had been designated for her, she knew she could never say no. The infant's name was Su Zhenzhen, and she was in Suzhou, a city located halfway between Shanghai and Nanjing. The "Su" in her name—the name all the adoptive families' daughters had been given—was for Suzhou. The "Zhenzhen," Myra learned, was Mandarin for "treasure."

Myra was due to travel one month later to pick up Zhenzhen—

whom she had decided to name Sadie, after her maternal grandmother—but a Chinese government travel approval was delayed. Finally, ten weeks later, in October, approval came through. Myra continues the story:

"Of the eight families in our group, five were couples and three were single women. I brought a close friend, Nan, who had good infant-care skills. I have to admit that some of my memories of the first few days are a blur now. I brought a journal with me and wrote a detailed account of my experiences prior to getting Sadie, but once I had her, the writing became erratic. The families, who made their own arrangements to travel to China, assembled in Shanghai under the leadership of a wonderful guide hired by our agency, and we were driven by van to Suzhou.

"The first inkling that I was soon to become a mother came when Nan and I entered our hotel room. There, in addition to the twin beds, was a tiny crib. It felt surreal to realize that the next night my daughter would be sleeping in it. We would meet our daughters the next morning.

"With still cameras and camcorders in hand, we waited in the lobby to see our daughters come in. At around 9:00 A.M., a van arrived and in it was the director of the welfare home and four young female caregivers, each carrying two babies. They sat on sofas that faced each other with the little girls. What a moment! The videocameras whirred, and we whispered curiously, trying to figure out which baby belonged to whom. Some had changed little from their photos, but I couldn't pick out Sadie right away, even though I'd carried around her picture for three and a half months. I first made eye contact with a little girl who was destined for someone else. Sadie turned out to be the other child being held by the same caregiver. She had a full head of hair and a grumpy expression.

"I was soon handed ten-month-old Su Zhenzhen, who clutched my upper arms and rested her head firmly on my chest. I have thought about this moment over and over. A photo shows me on the verge of tears and Sadie looking frightened. At that moment, she lost everything in her short life that was familiar to her: her Chinese caregivers, the sounds, the smells, the buildings, and the rhythms that had made up her life. It was as though she had been abandoned for a second time. I brought her upstairs and placed her on a bed, wondering what to do next. I didn't have to wonder for long: she promptly fell into a deep sleep. While other families were changing their daughters' clothes and feeding them, Sadie napped. If ever there was love at first sight, this wasn't it.

"Within two days, however, it became clear that Sadie was a robust baby with a great appetite. She promptly earned the nicknames 'The Tank' for her sturdy body and 'La Boca' for her big mouth! And she bonded to me surprisingly fast."

On October 14, 1996, Myra Alperson and Sadie Zhenzhen became a family.

Eight weeks later, having returned home, Myra reported: "Sadie is very much a cuddler, very much at home in New York City playgrounds, and she has been lovingly welcomed at my synagogue. She has given so much to me in the short time that we have known each other, and I marvel several times a day at the remarkable process that matched this middle-aged New York Jewish woman with a precious daughter from China."

Myra Alperson, besides being the mother of Sadie, is an award-winning journalist who specializes in studying the relationship between business and society. She is a senior research associate at The Conference Board, in New York City.